The **RANDORI PRINCIPLES**

THE PATH OF EFFORTLESS LEADERSHIP

David Baum | *Jim Hassinger*

Dearborn™
Trade Publishing
A **Kaplan Professional** Company

Senior Acquisitions Editor: Jean Iversen
Senior Managing Editor: Jack Kiburz
Interior Design: Lucy Jenkins
Cover Design: Scott Rattray, Rattray Design
Typesetting: Elizabeth Pitts

Published by Dearborn Trade Publishing, a Kaplan Professional Company

Library of Congress Cataloging-in-Publication Data

Baum, David.
    The Randori principles : the path to effortless leadership / David Baum, James Hassinger.
        p.   cm.
    ISBN 0-7931-4862-6 (5.5 × 8.5 hardcover)
    1. Leadership—Japan. 2. Management—Japan. 3. Aikido.   I. Hassinger, James.   II. Title.
    HD57.7 .B385 2002
    658.4'092—dc21   2001006187

DAVID'S DEDICATION

To my brother Larry, my first and best *randori* partner. I used to beat you up. Now, no more.

JIM'S DEDICATION

To my children, Kelsey and Sam. It is their generation who will need the *randori principles* the most.

FOREWORD

Randori \ran-'door-ee\ *vb* (from the Japanese martial art aikido) means to be in the right place, with the right technique, at the right time, with the right level of power. In this book, authors David Baum and Jim Hassinger illustrate how *randori* is an important and apt metaphor for the challenge of leadership in the 21st century.

For many people, the ideals of the Industrial Revolution —the never-ending desire for more progress, more development, and greater wealth—no longer seem relevant, yet we have trouble letting them go. If we are to survive in the world of the 21st century, however, we must consider priorities.

Through his analysis of the rise and fall of 20 civilizations, the great historian Arnold Toynbee offers a larger perspective on the current shifts in values and lifestyles. Summarizing the principles of civilization growth, Toynbee formulated the Law of Progressive Simplification, which reminds us that the measure of a civilization's growth and sustainable vitality lies in its ability to transfer increasing amounts of energy and attention from the material side of life to the educational, psychological, cultural, aesthetic, and spiritual sides.

To make this kind of shift, supporting Toynbee's Law of Progressive Simplification, people must become more capable of handling change than ever before. Indigenous and

Eastern cultures have long recognized that the only constant
in our lives is change, and that the principles of interdepen-
dence and sustainable vitality are essential for growth and
survival. What are the choices and consequences for which
we currently must take responsibility or whose course we
must correct? How can we meet the challenge of our times?

Essentially, our collective challenge is to use the metaphor of *randori* actively and to become "change masters"—a
term Rosabeth Moss Kanter introduced in 1985. How can
we become change masters who support progressive simplification and make choices that sustain values of courage, integrity, responsibility, creativity, humor, wisdom, and love?

Continuity and integration of social change cannot be
accomplished without the support of an appropriate con-
sciousness among people. Leadership may be human nature's
oldest consciousness-raising act that is designed to foster and
stabilize individual and collective awareness and health during times of change and transition. An effective change master today recognizes that *randori* is an invaluable tool for
integrating changes and maintaining healthy human beings.

American writer Charles Reich reinforces the need for
effective leadership when he argues that a society is mad when
its actions are no longer guided by what will make people
healthier and happier; when its power is no longer in service
of life. Tribal people recognize that no positive change is
sustained or integrated without ritualized rites of passage or
effective council processes and collaboration. *Randori*—a
full-powered presence—ultimately creates a bridge between inner and outer worlds, reconnecting us with the seat of our

souls to better serve ourselves and others in healthier, more effective ways.

The conscious use of *randori,* with unwavering commitment to character development and spiritual work in organizations, business, and communities, mobilizes us to become true change masters who actually build sustainable bridges between many worlds. It is very important for us to take our place, to bring our gifts and talents forward to shift the shape of our reality, and to build new worlds both internally and externally that allow for our civilization's growth to align with the Law of Progressive Simplification. This is all that is needed to support the realm of spirit or mastery in all aspects of our lives.

—Angeles Arrien, cultural anthropologist and author of *The Four-Fold Way* and *Signs of Life*

CONTENTS

Acknowledgments xiii

Introduction xvii

SECTION ONE

RANDORI
GREAT RESULTS WITH MINIMAL STRUGGLE

Randori in Business 3

At Black Belt, You've Just Begun 6

SECTION TWO

FULL-POWERED PRESENCE
LEADERSHIP WORTH FOLLOWING

What Is *Full-Powered Presence?* 13

The Speed of Breath 17

Fill Your Energy Field 20

Wu Wei: Find the Effortless Path 25

The Two Sides of Presence 31

Stay Unattached to Outcome 35

Tune into Your Radar 39

The Trap of Inflation 44

The Trap of Denial 47

Avoiding the Tyranny of Immediacy 51

A Vice-Grip Is Not Your Only Tool in Life 55

Truisms Are Not Truth 59

The Power of Ritual 63

Help Others to Get Back into Presence 67

SECTION THREE

TENKAN
TURNING RESISTANCE INTO COLLABORATION

What Is *Tenkan?* 75
Get Off the Firing Line 79
Get Close to Your Attacker 84
Join with Your Adversary 87
Take Someone's Balance 90
Attack the Ebbs 94
Kill the Enemy 99
Count on Silence 103
Share the Pain 107
A Short Natural History of Fear and Resistance 111
Forget about Change, Worry about Transition 114
Separate the Past from the Future 117
Death and Renewal 121

SECTION FOUR

IRIMI
THE SINGLE SWORD STRIKE

What Is *Irimi?* 123
The Three Irimi Techniques 128
Keep the Strike Simple 130
Boldly Seize the Teachable Moment 134
Create the Compelling Decision 138
Speak Your Truth without Blame or Judgment 142
Get Unstuck through Penalty 147
Verbal *Atemi:* The "Wake-Up Call" Response 152
The Two Essentials to Movement 156
The Find Line of Giving Advice 159

The Power of True Apology   164
The Street Muggers in Your Meeting   167
Humility Keeps Us Connected When Using Power   173
Answer Your Calling   177

SECTION FIVE

GET OFF THE MAT
THE SKILL OF DISENGAGEMENT

What Is *Get Off the Mat?*   185
Our Fears Are Always Strongest before We Let Go   188
Relationships as a Reason, Season, or Lifetime   192
If You're Locked into Control, It's a Good Idea to Get
   Off the Mat   196
Get Off the Mat of Your Calendar   200
Lead from the Shadows   204
Disengagement: the Art of Taking No Action   207
Unplug from Power Struggles   211
Let Go of What You Create   216

SECTION SIX

MOVING TO ADVANCED RANDORI
MASTERING LEADERSHIP

The Dance of Advanced Randori Leadership   223
Develop a Warrior's Soul   225
Leader as Worthy Adversary   228
Effortless and Sustainable   233
Today's Leadership Skills Won't Be Good Enough
   Tomorrow   238
Avoid Overdependence on Leadership   241
Take a Deep Dive into Effortless Leadership   245

Suggested Reading List   249

ACKNOWLEDGMENTS

DAVID'S ACKNOWLEDGMENTS

In writing this book, many voices supported my efforts. The following appreciations are in order.

To O'Sensei for his extraordinary life. I bow deeply to your memory.

To my significant teachers of spirit: Angeles Arrien and Virginia McKenzie, who at various times in my life helped me to understand the connection between theory and real life. And when needed, smacked me upside my head.

To all those clients who let me practice what I preached as I was writing this book. In particular, I want to thank William Oullin at Barclays Bank, Jonathan Coslet at The Texas Pacific Group, Doug Ayer of Coldwell Banker, Rick Little and Bill Reese at The International Youth Foundation, Jerry White at The Landmine Survivors Network, Sonia Madison at Health Partners, and Robin Moll at Main Line Health. I sincerely appreciate your support. Thank you.

To our editor at Dearborn Trade Publishing, Jean Iversen, for her extraordinary *atemi* skills when dealing with challenging authors.

To David and Cynthia Knudsen for providing a place in Canada of almost unbelievable inspiration and beauty.

To Rod Napier, who helped me hone my *randori* skills over many, many years of friendship.

To Chris Cappy, for his always illuminating conversations in personal and professional learning.

To Barbara, my office assistant, for keeping me off the mat of worry.

To so many unnamed sources of ongoing inspiration, specifically, in no particular order of appearance: William Bridges, Mathew Fox, Deidre Combs, Margaret Condon, Pamela Nelson, Julie Roberts, Kathy Karn, Elizabeth Murray, Amanda Assinway, Bonnie Kramer, Roger Low, and Ruby.

And finally, to my beloved wife, Terry, and stepchildren, Kate and Galen, who have been the fire without which nothing else matters.

JIM'S ACKNOWLEDGMENTS

I would like to express the deepest gratitude to my aikido teachers. The ongoing innovation and exploration by Richard Moon, Sensei, has been inspiring. I recommend his book, *Aikido in Three Easy Lessons*. Chris Thorsen, Sensei, has both pioneered and made significant contributions to the application of aikido in the business world, and he has been a role model in his dedication to that pursuit. I have benefited tremendously from their generosity, personal coaching, and friendship.

Professor Takeshi Sairenji, Shihan, and Stephen Kalil, Sensei, of Aikido of Worcester, have provided years of exceptional instruction. They have created a dojo that truly models the Founder's values of respect, humility, and friendship. Terry Dobson, in the brief time we knew each other, was also inspirational. His book, *It's a Lot Like Dancing,* is a beautiful testimony to the art of aikido. Finally, it is Morihei Ueshiba, O'Sensei, who deserves the most recognition for his wisdom in creating aikido, the way of harmony.

In addition, I would like to thank the many colleagues with whom I have shared the joy of aikido. In particular, my appreciation goes to Toby, Charlie, Ruth, Michael, Marilyn, and the Worcester Aikido dojo brothers. I am also grateful to my colleagues and clients who have supported the use of aikido principles in the business world. Most notably, I want to thank Sheila Carroll, Jamie Conglose, and John Strauss, as well as Barbara Kuby, Carol Schifman, Jeffrey MacGregor, Bob Madden, Chris Cappy, and Rich Amodio.

Off the mat, I am especially grateful to Angeles Arrien and Mo Maxfield for their teaching and personal coaching based in their Four Fold Way model of indigenous wisdom. Their insights have been most helpful, personally and professionally.

Other business colleagues and friends who have been helpful over the years have been Barry Carden, Nancy Cray, Allen Hollander, John Kerrick, Paul and Anne Nash, Mary Connaughton, Andrea Campbell, and Ellen Corcoran.

Chris Mann, in particular, has provided many insightful suggestions for this book, and her encouragement, support, and love have been most appreciated.

Our Dearborn editor, Jean Iversen, and her team provided the right balance of encouragement and helpful critique.

Finally, I would like to thank my parents and brother, Lee, Charlene, and Jon Hassinger, and my children, Kelsey and Sam, for their love and support over the years.

INTRODUCTION

Do nothing which is of no use.

—Musashi

What is *randori?*

Imagine this: You are alone on a martial arts practice mat surrounded by four attackers with swords. Suddenly, you are charged from multiple directions at once, seemingly with no pattern or predictability. Unrelenting and with full-out commitment, the simultaneous armed strikes keep coming. But instead of panicking or flailing or offering your head for a quick release from your body, you respond with inner calm and effortless movement. Each response, each technique you bring forward perfectly parries every force you encounter. You flow with the attacks, almost without thought, and in so doing diffuse the flurry of your opposition. After awhile your attackers become exhausted. Suddenly, their efforts appear pointless. It is clear that no matter what they do, you will stand unharmed. The session ends with a mutual bow of respect.

This is *randori.*

Randori \ran-'door-ee\ *vb* (from the Japanese martial art aikido) means to be in the right place, with the right technique, at the right time, with the right level of power.

In order to be able to perform *randori* one must have two skills. The first is the ability to learn and perform essential techniques from aikido that have stood the test of time. These are strategies and techniques from aikido that have proven enormously effective over many years of experience with multiple kinds of tests. Again and again, the learner must practice these essential skills until they are "in the bones"—part of the fabric of who and how this individual operates.

But *randori* is not defined as just knowing a series of techniques. Right response delivered at the wrong time or with too much power will generate unneeded resistance or confusion. Thus, the second skill of *randori* requires a heightened level of awareness. It is an ability to discern the perfect combination of timing and delivery that caters to the uniqueness of every situation with bold and decisive action. *Randori* requires personal mastery of one's leadership skills. And mastery is more than a menu of responses. It is having the discernment to know what techniques to use, when to use them, and what level of power is needed.

This is *randori*.

In some ways the metaphor is a perfect match for today's business environment. Consider a multi-billion-dollar global bank changing its customer model to one of market management, an international oil company implementing a new $200 million information system, a small foundation needing to respond to multiple simultaneous requests for funding, a health care system transforming its care delivery system in today's hostile reimbursement environment, or a financial ser-

vices company navigating a merger. These are all clients we
have worked with and, in doing so, have brought forward the
"spirit" of *randori*.

It is important to note that this is not a martial arts book,
the history of aikido, or the story of its brilliant founder,
Morihei Ueshiba, O'Sensei. There are many fine books on
these topics as well as senior aikido teachers who are more
qualified than we are to comment about aikido from a martial arts perspective. We have a great deal of respect for these
masters.

Our intention is different. Although the aikido stories
and examples come from Jim's experience, we wish to translate some of those learnings to the complex job of leading.
These lessons, which we call the *randori principles,* define a
path of effortless leadership that can create extraordinary
results. Other sources of wisdom, such as those from indigenous cultures as taught by the brilliant anthropologist,
Angeles Arrien, are also woven into this collection of leadership tactics that really work.

We base the book on the following four core concepts:

1. As with aikido, business leaders need to continually
   expand their repertoire of basic skills, like strategic
   planning, project management, giving performance
   feedback, managing cross-functional conflict, and
   communicating effectively in times of change. They
   need to practice these basic skills so their capabilities
   become second nature in application to a variety of
   situations.

2. Concurrently, a leader must also develop an ability to choose the right approach, with the right timing, and the appropriate use of power. Leadership should not rely on using a cookie-cutter approach to this fast-changing global business situation. Good judgment, part of which we call *randori*, is as valuable as core leadership skills.

3. Combine *randori* judgment and extensive leadership skill, and you find yourself on the path of effortless leadership. This is not to say that great leadership requires little or no effort. To the contrary, with the highest level of skill applied with perfect timing and power, you help eliminate the wasted time and energy that keep jobs from looking or feeling easy. And while few executives have actually lost their head in corporate battle, many have lost their jobs over the misuse of action, timing, or power.

4. The leadership path is only effortless if it is sustainable over time. Short bursts of leadership effectiveness appear brilliant, but if they are not based in the *randori principles*, then the leader and organization will quickly exhaust their resources. Most people or organizations cannot sustain an unrelenting top-speed activity pace. Focusing on making choices that are sustainable allows the organization to bypass inefficiency and struggle, creating a more effortless path to great results.

The payoff is significant: heightened awareness of possibilities, decisiveness that slices through tough business issues, effortless implementation, and outcomes that surpass your expectations. In over 40 years of collective experience with leaders, this is our short list of what just plain works. We know it. Our clients know it. And the results have proven to bear them out. On the "mat" of our client's business challenges, this book offers a collection of proven *randori* skills.

"OK," you say, "makes sense. So how do I learn the *randori principles* and put them into practice?"

The Randori Principles blends together nearly 60 short, accessible chapters—stories and lessons of what we know works. How, for instance, do you know when to apologize or when to just keep walking? Or, how do you neutralize a boss's direct attack in a meeting? Or, how do you create change through silence?

It is organized into six main sections—the key components of *randori*.

Section One is an overview of the philosophy of *randori* in action and how you as a leader can balance timing, effort, and action.

Section Two is called "Full-Powered Presence: Leadership Worth Following" and teaches about the different ways to bring your leadership fully forward without hesitation or compromise.

Section Three is called "Tenkan: Turning Resistance into Collaboration" and provides strategies for how you can transform challenging situations by minimizing resistance and struggle.

Section Four is called "Irimi: The Single Sword Strike" and teaches techniques for making a major impact in decisive and deliberate moves.

Section Five is called "Get Off the Mat: The Skill of Disengagement" and is a guide to identification and disengagement from overwhelming or dangerous leadership situations.

The final section provides advanced *randori* tactics.

The Randori Principles combines leadership lessons from aikido with cross-cultural knowledge that has been effectively used in the business world—all with great stories and immediately applicable lessons in a simple, straightforward format.

Pick it up anywhere. Read from any spot. If you find something useful, put it into practice. But above all else, use it as a looking glass to examine your own leadership abilities.

In aikido, when you are so present that all the techniques you know are evenly available to you, it is said: "The fight is over before it begins." We believe the same is true in business.

DB/JH

RANDORI

GREAT RESULTS WITH MINIMAL STRUGGLE

RANDORI IN BUSINESS

There is no need to struggle to be free;
the absence of struggle is in itself freedom.

—Chogyan Trungpa

In the martial art of aikido, people practice in pairs, with one partner providing a specific attack and the other practicing the aikido response. After several repetitions, they switch roles. To really master a technique requires understanding it from both sides of the relationship. Once you know some basic skills, multiple attackers are used to elevate the skill of technique selection, timing, and power. Think *Crouching Tiger, Hidden Dragon*.

When two or three people attack simultaneously and from different directions and with varied strikes, you don't have much time to carefully plan out your response. By the time you have gone through that thought process, the other attackers have hit their mark. Your success depends on two factors: (1) your repertoire of techniques to handle different attacks and (2) your ability to stay calm while under pressure, so that you can choose the appropriate counterattack with just the right timing and power.

There are wristlocks, hip throws, and sword thrusts, for example. Perfecting just one technique takes years of practice, so that you can precisely perform a specific series of movements to neutralize an attack and make it look easy. But just because you know several hundred or a thousand techniques doesn't mean that you will be effective on the mat. Choose the wrong response or use too much force in applying the technique, and it will feel like a struggle. Respond too early, and your attacker will change his or her strike; too late, and the force of his or her attack will be too strong to neutralize. So you have to combine your selection of just the right technique with a perfect sense of timing and appropriate level of power.

You learn a lot in multiple-attacker practice sessions. Overanalyzing the incoming attack slows down your response time. Too much focus on one attacker, and you lose sight of your other adversaries. Respond halfheartedly, and it takes too long to dismiss one attacker, leaving you vulnerable to the others. Use too much force, and you get entangled. Freeze up out of fear or indecision, and all three attackers simultaneously declare victory. Gloat for a moment after effectively handling that hard punch to the stomach, and you lose track of that strike to the back of your head.

Now picture this leadership scenario: There is a moment as a leader when everything just clicks. You are able to quickly make sense of a complex situation, discerning the right course of action from myriad options. The timing of your decision couldn't be better, and your organization is open to your guidance. Your team usually requires boatloads of rationale before they are willing to change, but your up-front work with them has neutralized that resistance. Your boss, typically absent because of his global responsibilities, responds to your request to attend your kickoff meeting and demonstrates political support of the new change. Onstage, you say just the right things, with a combination of ease and passion that creates a compelling message. In spite of the monumental task, with all its risks and long hours, you find your leadership role to be rather effortless, in fact invigorating. Most of your colleagues thought you'd be exhausted or eaten up by the politics by now.

This scenario describes *randori* effortless leadership in the business world. Perfect timing and approach and little to no resistance from the organization in challenging situations create great results with relatively little effort. The following essential techniques rest at the heart of this style. Try these to start developing your *randori* leadership skills:

1. Effortless leadership requires a balance of taking fully committed action without hesitation or deliberately choosing not to act. There is a perfect timing of events, or *wu wei,* and following that natural order minimizes struggle and inefficient use of resources.

2. In order to discern the perfect timing of events and lead effortlessly, you need to be at *full-powered presence. Full-powered presence* requires relaxed readiness, open-mindedness, and high energy sustainable over time.

3. The skill of *tenkan* enables you to deeply understand your colleagues while avoiding adversarial attacks. Dissipating resistance and quickly resolving conflicts paves the way to smooth implementation of business plans.

4. *Irimi* provides an approach to slice through to the core of a business issue and take decisive action.

Through well-timed use of humor, apology, silence, or advice, to name a few, *irimi* leadership techniques balance boldness and compassion.

5. Right timing and right placement emphasize the option to take no action in order to conserve vital organizational resources. *Randori* would also suggest that there are some interactions it is wiser to disengage from, or to metaphorically get off the mat, than to continue participating in a power struggle.

The *randori principles* provide a blueprint for leaders to discern the best path for their organization, effortlessly implement those plans with the least struggle and resistance, and in the process, create extraordinary results.

JH

AT BLACK BELT, YOU'VE JUST BEGUN

It takes a minimum of ten years to master the basics.
Never think of yourself as all knowing.
Today's techniques will be different tomorrow.

—O'Sensei

There are 20 basic techniques in aikido that beginners learn to use in responding to different attacks. There are 6,000 variations of those core techniques. Even after studying aikido for ten years, there could still be techniques you have yet to learn. To reach a level of Black Belt, you need to progress through six levels of skill development. To be awarded the rank of Black Belt is a high honor. What is equally daunting is that there are ten more levels of Black Belt to attain after reaching that rank.

Often it is said that when you reach Black Belt, you finally understand the basics and can really begin to learn the art of aikido. Some of the highest-ranking teachers in the world comment that after practicing a certain technique for 30 years, they feel they are just beginning to get it. There is a deep respect and awe for the vastness of the art of aikido by those who make their study a lifetime practice.

What if the art of leadership were viewed in the same way?

There are certain core skills that a leader needs to develop in order to handle the day-to-day tasks. The list might include capabilities in giving performance feedback, managing a project, putting together a plan, or interviewing candidates. Organizations develop competency lists of skill and knowledge areas that are important for all managers to have in order for the company to be successful. In the best cases, training programs are offered and coaching provided to those managers.

Learning the basics is similar to progressing through the six ranks to the rank of Black Belt. After that, the focus becomes the refinement of those skills with a variety of different people and different situations. What subtle approaches should be used in communicating to investment managers that would not be effective with field sales? How would you change your coaching style with a new employee compared to a seasoned one? How much detail should you communicate after a merger has been announced but before closing?

As you master the basics, you can focus on adding additional techniques to your repertoire as you gain experience with a variety of situations. Approaching the art of leadership with the same high level of interest and conviction that you did when you were a first-time supervisor, you become known as a resource to other managers. Other managers will come to you for advice about how to handle a certain employee problem or ask you to help them plan a critical meeting.

Too often in organizations, the people with the biggest titles are assumed to be fully skilled as leaders, not in need of further training, and highly capable at their present level. Just because they now have the title of vice president doesn't mean they know everything there is to know about leading. In reality, after completing a training course, most managers will ask why their boss hasn't taken the program, because they need the skill as well. Ask any CEO, and he will tell you that the higher you go up the corporate ladder, the less feedback you get. Unless he enrolls in the two-month university executive programs, his development has stopped. What's worse is that many top executives have taken a fast-track promotion path and sorely lack some of the basic leadership skills.

Randori emphasizes the long view on leadership development. Learning the basics is comparable to getting your Black Belt, after which the real mastery process begins. What if organizations not only defined their competency model, but also encouraged employees to continue to refine their skills at ten levels beyond the basics? What if companies had master leaders whose job it was to coach, mentor, and teach the more advanced and subtle techniques of leadership? What if the role of manager or leader represented a symbol of skill and knowledge, rather than a title given to justify an increase of compensation? What if every manager approached his job with the same high level of commitment and humility on his first day as in his 20th year as a leader?

The implication is important. As a leader, never assume that success means you can stop growing and developing. The opposite is true. With the position comes a greater responsibility to continue to add to your repertoire. After all, the higher you rise in your organization, the more people you impact. The *randori principles* suggest that even when faced with intense pressures on the job, great leaders still strive for self-assessment and ongoing learning. A leader who stops learning is one who will eventually end up in trouble and doing harm—either to himself or others. A true master never stops learning. For that matter neither does a true leader.

TRY THIS . . .

- Identify three advanced leadership skills or knowledge areas that all managers need to have in order for your organization to be successful.

- Evaluate yourself against these criteria and fill any gaps.

- Provide learning opportunities to build those capabilities for leaders in your organization.

JH

FULL-POWERED PRESENCE

LEADERSHIP WORTH FOLLOWING

WHAT IS FULL-POWERED PRESENCE?

Roots of a large summer tree

On a rock.

Extend in all directions.

—Kyoshi Takahama

A good day on the mat has certain characteristics: At the end of class, you feel more energized than when you started. You handled a variety of attacks with grace and power, feeling competent in the skills you have worked hard to learn. Practicing with your usual adversary seems much more effortless this time. Even when your timing is off or a new move doesn't neutralize a strike, you value the learning, both about the aikido technique and about yourself. You might have a tendency to rush through tasks at work, and you did the same thing in that last attack. There's an uplifting mood on the mat—high energy, laughter, and impeccable spirit. If only every day at work had the same results.

A good day on the mat depends primarily on the ability to be at *full-powered presence* for the whole class. It has less to do with your skill level.

There is a story frequently told in aikido circles about a skilled samurai swordsman. One day he unknowingly challenges a man in battle who turns out to be a master of the Japanese tea ceremony. Although the tea master knows little of sword technique, his presence, impeccable integrity, and inclusive power completely dissolve the samurai's will to attack. The samurai warrior quickly admits defeat, because the tea master provides no openings for attack. His discipline and focus prove too much for the samurai, and the "battle" is momentary. Without ever picking up a weapon, the tea master has peacefully resolved the conflict. This is what being at *full-powered presence* is all about.

Full-powered presence allows you to be at your best, handle new and unknown situations, and respond effortlessly to the challenges of work. It complements the core leadership skills and magnetizes commitment and loyalty from direct reports. It gives leaders the capability to manage a project, even though they are not experts in that function. *Full-powered presence* gives leaders the skill to address resistance or challenges from colleagues with grace, tact, and decisiveness. Maintaining high energy levels and sustaining focus in fast-changing business environments emanate from *full-powered presence*.

Full-powered presence requires the following attitudes and skills:

1. Relaxed readiness describes your physical state. You have high energy but not the tension that strenuous sports might require. Nor are you so relaxed that you won't be able to respond in an instant. You adopt a neutral way of sitting or standing, not aggressively leaning in or passively held back.

2. Your breathing style helps deepen and ground your relaxed readiness. Longer and continuous breathing cycles help calm us and, according to Eastern beliefs, give us access to *ki,* a universal source of extra energy.

Picture filling your lungs and then breathing further into your abdomen. Your breathing helps you center and helps infuse a calm and focused tone in a meeting.

3. Mentally, you are calm and alert, while being open to input and other perspectives. Unattached to outcome describes the attitude of creating options without prematurely converging to a decision. On the other hand, you value and are capable of making a decision swiftly with full commitment. Being preoccupied with other thoughts works against being at *full-powered presence.*

4. Emotionally well balanced describes someone at *full-powered presence.* This person takes responsibility for her actions and expresses her feelings honestly and without blame. She can get some distance in heated issues, so that she doesn't take things personally. Seeing the larger worldview in any situation, she relishes times of complexity and controversy as opportunities to make important changes. Realistic about her own strengths and weaknesses, her self-confidence and comfort with a wide range of different personalities seems to set others at ease.

5. *Full-powered presence* is a lifetime practice. Impossible to achieve all the time, it is more effective to notice when you are off center or "minus" in your energy and then make adjustments to return to *full-powered presence.*

This is the foundation from which other *randori* leadership tactics can be applied. From *full-powered presence,* you have the perspective to make decisions about right approach, right timing, and right use of power. As we will describe later in the book, it is from that vantage point that other *tenkan* or *irimi* leadership techniques are best employed. With *full-powered presence,* a leader can walk into a room and before they have said a word, set the tone for collaboration, bold decision making, and effortless results.

TRY THIS . . .

- At the start of each day, identify one upcoming situation where being at *full-powered presence* will be important to your success.

- Mentally make a note or mark "FPP" next to that event in your calendar.

- Focus on the traits of *full-powered presence* before starting that engagement and review your success afterwards.

JH

THE SPEED OF BREATH

I've got to keep breathing.
It will be my worst business mistake if I don't.

—Sir Nathan Rothschild

Sheila was at a very intense meeting. She was in charge of assessing the viability of a merger candidate and putting the transition plan together if and when the deal went through. At the table were representatives of both companies. To say the tone was adversarial was an understatement. Everyone was feeling the pressure of making a huge decision in an incredibly short time frame. The window for this deal closed the next day. It was now or never—and big money and big egos were at stake. The two companies were quite different in their culture, history, and market approach, which only added to the tension. Fear, paranoia, impatience, and aggravation were the main ingredients of the day.

As soon as the meeting started, individuals rushed to dominate the conversation. The room was filled with four or five people talking at the same time. There was little or no listening or collaboration. The whole deal was going to hell in a handbasket. Those not involved in the battle checked out by turning away from the table or gazing at their cell phones for messages.

Sheila could feel the urgency and desire to take action, any action, consuming the group. She knew she had to do something different or else she would be pulled into the downward spiraling meeting. Trying to talk over the group wouldn't work, and shouting would only escalate the conflict.

As a way to disengage from the chaos, she decided to try something antithetical to her instinct to speed ahead. She did something very simple instead. She slowed down her breathing. That was it. All she did was focus on her breath. While others around her were nearly hyperventilating in activity, Sheila instead chose to quiet her internal pace. After a few moments, when she felt calm and focused, she leaned forward and began to intently listen. Even though she could track several conversations at once, Sheila chose to pay attention to only one speaker at a time. When she did speak, she was then able to integrate the multiple ideas around the table and bridge the two groups. She began to find the common ground that was elusive to anyone else.

More important than her helpful ideas, however, was the tone she conveyed. In a very subtle way, other team members seemed to pick up on her calm presence and non-reactive stance. One by one, they eased back into their chairs and off their aggressive posturing. Frenetic discussions quieted into the team focusing on a single topic. Within ten minutes of a very chaotic start, the due diligence team was able to converge their best thinking into some important recommendations.

This entire dramatic shift occurred very subtly. If you were sitting in the room, you would not have heard Sheila change her breathing pace, although you might have noticed her calm voice and her attentive listening. Chances are that you would not have seen Sheila try to take over the group with an aggressive bid for power in the midst of chaos. Instead, you would have witnessed a dramatic change in energy and atmosphere as the group was about ready to run out of oxygen, trying to be heard in the fray.

One Eastern perspective is that you are born with a certain number of breaths, and when you use them up, you die. Accordingly, this idea places value on an elongated breathing cycle that savors each breath. To elongate your breathing cycle, fill both your lungs *and* abdomen. Western conventional thinking says a normal breath cycle takes about 5 seconds (or 12 breaths per minute). However, a warrior about to engage in battle will hold the standard of one breath per minute, or one 25-second inhale followed by a 35-second exhale. Holding your breath as a shortcut to get to a minute doesn't count. It is one long, continuous effort.

Full-powered presence teaches us that when we elongate our breathing cycle, our thinking expands and our awareness of other people and dynamics increases. Fast-paced breathing tends to accentuate only our mental processes and to discourage the blending of analytical and intuitive ways of making decisions. When we are breathless, we are less centered and thus become more frenetic. The consequence is that uncentered leaders frequently become impatient, leaping to any action, without careful discernment. Thus, in a very real way, your style of breathing is directly related to your effectiveness as a leader.

So the next time you are feeling "breathless" at a meeting, rather than leaping to action, try to slow your breath instead. See what quieting the internal mind does to finding common ground and building collaboration. There is a difference between speed and frenzy. Slowing your breathing, just when you think you can't, is a terrific way to ensure the first and avoid the second.

TRY THIS . . .

- Each day, practice elongating your breathing cycle.

- In a pressure situation, use breathing to increase your effectiveness.

JH

FILL YOUR ENERGY FIELD

Even a wild boar
With all other things
Blew in this storm.

—Bashō

I have only "time traveled" a few times on the mat. Each time, I was standing, providing an attack to the sensei, and the next second, I was flat on my back with my teacher checking if I was OK. I have no memory of going from vertical to horizontal. It's as if someone edited out that part of the videotape from my brain. Metaphorically speaking, I was still thinking about getting my tickets while the rest of me had finished the train trip.

My first response was to elevate my already high level of respect for the skill of the sensei. I knew the sensei was good, but to accomplish these aikido techniques in such blinding speed was truly awesome. It was one thing to watch but quite another to experience the sensei's skill firsthand. Was perfecting the skill the secret of such mastery?

Senseis Richard Moon and Chris Thorsen point out that it is not just their skillful aikido response. In order for that speed to occur, the attacker must also leave an energetic void for such a fast counterattack to occur.

Energy void is an unusual term. Let me explain. In that moment of my attack, I was tentative, feeling on the spot in front of 75 fellow students and a bit anxious of what might happen to me at the hands of a highly skilled sensei. Like a balloon only half inflated, my lack of full confidence had diminished my ability to muster all my physical resources. My teacher sensed this and, like a hot knife through butter, was able to execute a split-second counter technique, all because of the energy void I had left him.

Senseis Moon and Thorsen talk about how the same energy dynamic often happens at the workplace. Picture each colleague having an energy field that expands and contracts depending on the situation. For instance, someone who is confident, energetic, and connected to everyone in a meeting would have a large energy field. Another person who is distracted or unsure might have a much smaller field. If someone is trying to take out his work frustrations on another, then his energy may have an aggressive edge to it. Compare that to the collaborative and creative feel emanating from someone who has just brought an exciting new product idea for the team to discuss.

The larger your energy field, the less vulnerable you are to the attacks or influences of others. The tendency is to gravitate to individuals emanating enthusiasm and confidence that feel inclusive. Charisma is one example of this magnetic quality that people want to be part of. In contrast, bravado tends to exclude or create distance, resulting in others stepping back rather than towards the leader.

On the other hand, an energy void presents an opportunity for others to fill it. Remember, nature abhors a vacuum. Unfortunately, a void does not discriminate between incoming energy based on good intentions or energy motivated by manipulative or self-serving needs. In one case, your colleague will notice you're having an off day and offer assistance. In another, you will be a potential victim. Your best approach is to keep your energy field as expansive as possible.

Creating a large energy field has different components. A positive attitude is certainly important. This means emphasizing confidence in your capabilities and your ability to deal with the unknown. Add to this a high level of physical energy. Relaxing your muscles and elongating your breathing expands your field; shallow breathing and tensing up deflates it. Picture a balloon that can be fully expanded, buoyant with some flexibility in the outer surface. You want your physical energy the same way, not underinflated nor overinflated. As the sensei suggests, try to imagine filling the room with your energy in a way that includes everyone at the table. That gives you *full-powered presence* while avoiding an energetic void.

As you pay attention, you will begin to notice what mental and physical conditions deflate your field. Fear and doubt reduce energy fields. Trying to control the situation with force adds an aggressive edge and narrows your field. Overly accommodating someone else's request creates a soft spot or vulnerability in your energy.

Your goal through daily practice is to easily create a fully extended energy field that invites your colleagues to join you in respectful, productive interaction. When both partners bring this quality of energy, the result is highly engaging, exhilarating work highlighted with fun, spontaneity, and great results. Neither person holds back, yet nobody is undermined. It is as if the full energy field that is cocreated makes a safe container, allowing creativity, genuine expression, and heartfelt connection.

Finally, your energy will magnetize similar energy. If you are positive, well intended, and robust, you will tend to draw similar responses from your colleagues. If you are fearful, you will draw attacks. Controlling or stubborn attitudes magnetize overly aggressive or passive-aggressive reactions. Even the most frustrated and aggressive opponent will gradually shift when in contact with someone who is respectful, open to creating mutually satisfying outcomes, and leaves no opening for attack.

One client, Lauren, continually found herself overloaded with too many projects. Wanting to be customer responsive, she would eventually say "yes" to far more tasks than were realistic for her to accomplish. Lauren realized that when clients started to make requests, she didn't want to disappoint them by saying "no." At the same time, she became anxious about meeting these unrealistic expectations. She started shrinking away from the table, almost hiding behind her notepad. All this contributed to narrowing her energy field and encouraged the client to add even more requests.

She principally remedied the overbooking situation through expanding her energy field when she was with clients. Attitudinally, she shifted to the perspective that creating false hopes or making promises she couldn't deliver was more harmful than saying "no" at the outset. Energywise, she emanated enthusiasm and confidence about the options, but tempered her message with a flavor of being grounded rather than rushing to "yes." Her clients noticed the difference and slowed down their pace of requests, even apologizing for past unrealistic delivery expectations. As a result, her clients' satisfaction increased, and Lauren was able to deliver consistent results over time, while feeling more comfortable in the project planning meetings.

Full-powered presence teaches us that the quality of our energy is a subtle but important criterion to our successful interactions with other people. Emanating a large, inclusive energy field encourages exhilarating, creative work and keeps us from creating a void.

TRY THIS . . .

- Identify someone who zaps your energy field, leaving a void with which they can unfairly influence.

- The next time you make contact with this person, pay attention to the quality of your attention and energy.

- Make adjustments so that you are focused, at full energy, and emanating a spirit of cooperation.

JH

WU WEI: FIND THE EFFORTLESS PATH

Dwell as near as possible to the channel in which your life flows.

—Henry David Thoreau

I was in New York City recently working with a client, and from the moment my plane touched down, I was immersed in the crush of humanity—through the terminal, in the cab stuck in traffic forever, jammed like sardines in the elevators, and, most pronounced, dodging and weaving on the crowded streets. How does anyone get where they're going in one piece and with peace of mind?

It was then that I was reminded of a story about O'Sensei, the founder of aikido. It was told to me one night at my kitchen table by Terry Dobson, one of the first Americans to study with him. Terry Dobson was a big man, large enough to try out for a linebacker position on the New York Giants football team. O'Sensei was five foot, one inch and in his later years. Terry was one of O'Sensei's senior students and personal assistants who attended to his needs when they traveled together to meet foreign dignitaries or conduct an aikido demonstration.

On this particular day, Terry and O'Sensei were to take a train to another city and unfortunately had to travel during rush hour. Apparently, rush hour in Japan makes New York City look like a ghost town, because after waiting forever to get their tickets, Terry took one look over the top of the jam-packed terminal and knew his linebacker skills would come in handy. He told O'Sensei their departure track and said to stick closely behind him, because he was going to plow through the crowd like Moses parting the Red Sea. Using his suitcases like a snowplow and his booming voice like a siren, Terry was determined to clear a path for his aged teacher. In spite of his determination and his formidable presence, progress was slow. There just wasn't any room for pedestrians to go.

At one point, Terry glanced behind him to reassure O'Sensei and update him on their progress. After all, standing a good foot over the rest of the crowd afforded him a perspective that his much shorter teacher did not have. Much to his horror, Terry could not find O'Sensei. This was not good. It was his sole responsibility to attend to O'Sensei, and he had lost him in the train station. How would he possibly find him among what seemed to be several thousand people? The poor man was probably trampled by now.

With life-and-death urgency, Terry plowed through the crowd towards their train. Sweat poured down his face and, just as he was about to yell for help from the conductor, he noticed O'Sensei calmly standing on board the train.

"Terry, are you all right? I was beginning to worry about you," exclaimed O'Sensei.

Terry, tremendously relieved and at the same time perplexed, asked, "O'Sensei, how did you survive the crowd? How could you possibly have gotten here any faster than I did? The crowd was so thick, and it was impossible to move people out of the way."

O'Sensei smiled and went on to talk about *his* perspective. He described entering the crowd, pausing for a moment to watch the different people, their energy, and pace. The frenetic chaos had a rhythm of its own, and when matched to the pattern of movement, all sorts of openings were created. The path to the train turned out to be quite effortless and enjoyable. O'Sensei had observed that Terry was too focused on plowing through the crowd to notice the easy route. "Now, let's get you on board and help you cool down with some water," was O'Sensei's comment as he eased Terry onto the train.

Particularly when in the midst of chaos, many of us put our heads down and just focus on plowing through a project. Guts, persistence, and self-discipline are important character traits to bring to bear on a task but can lead to a narrow perspective. Without stepping back from a project, it's hard to notice the *wu wei,* or perfect flow, of people, activity, timing, and energy.

In aikido and Eastern cultures, there is a term called *wu wei. Wu wei* represents the perfect flow of events, and it is one of the keys to effortless leadership. The perfect flow of events is not always linear or predictable. It certainly isn't fast all the time. Those leaders who choose to pay attention to *wu wei* know that there is a natural ebb and flow to any endeavor, and the secret is to align yourself and your organization to that rhythm.

Wu wei suggests that there is a right moment to act, and waiting for that moment provides an effortless path. To move too quickly or too late requires more effort, and part of leadership is sensing the right moment to take action. Most leaders try to force the timing of events because of an overdependence on schedules and an overreliance on persistence. Corporate America thrives on last-minute heroics, but it has a cost.

Some cues to find the effortless path are found in hints such as these from Eastern culture:

- In bad times, be slow; in good times, be fast.

- Deliberate slowly; act promptly.

- The best action may be no action.

They suggest that there is a balance between focused, committed, deliberate action and openness to timing that transcends the project. Put the project plan together, including the GANT chart that anticipates multitasking. Back-solve a project so that you know exactly how long each task will take and when you need to initiate the next. *Wu wei* doesn't suggest that you abandon good organization or planning for reckless spontaneity.

Instead, take your thinking to another level by viewing your plan from the path of least resistance. What will be re-

quired for the plan to be effortlessly executed? Are there unnecessary complexities built into the design that will
overconsume the team's resources? Have the political implications been thought of and potential struggles avoided? Are
team members all of a sudden overloaded with other responsibilities that are siphoning off their creative energy or has an
opening been created that clears the path to an unusually
high spurt of productivity? Are customer preferences changing and are you paying attention to their subtle clues? Is the
timing so perfect that it warrants pulling people off other
projects and seizing a fleeting competitive advantage with a
customer?

Once you have started the implementation of your plan,
continue paying attention to *wu wei*. Sometimes projects go
seamlessly according to plan, and other times they seem
doomed from the beginning. In those moments when patience and perseverance are tested, it may make sense to conserve your energy and put a task aside. On the aikido mat,
some days you feel like you have forgotten everything you
know and can't do any techniques right. Every interaction
feels like a struggle, and your timing is way off. Those are
times to slow down and readjust your expectations. Sometimes, it's best to just stop practicing and watch instead. The
path of least resistance is not just taking the easy way out. It
is finding the path that paves the way for great results with
minimal struggle.

Full-powered presence teaches us to be aware of *wu wei*,
the perfect timing of events. When nothing seems to be
working, the best decision may be to dramatically *shift your*

expectations for the day and even clear your schedule. It might be better to put the project on hold or even take the day off to rejuvenate. On the other hand, when the path opens up, bring all your resources to bear on the task, for you never know how long the window of opportunity will be open. Above all, trust that there is a perfect order of events that, although discouraging at the moment, may in retrospect reveal hidden blessings.

Full-powered presence teaches us to first slow down long enough to see the effortless path in the midst of chaos. Otherwise, you can exhaust yourself pursuing a goal and arrive having lost what matters most.

TRY THIS . . .

- Review three of your projects for *wu wei* timing.

- Are they proceeding effortlessly and with appropriate timing?

- Should you accelerate the pace and allocate more resources to some?

- Is putting others on hold the right choice right now?

JH

THE TWO SIDES OF PRESENCE

Nothing is worth more than this day.

—Goethe

The other day I attended the memorial service of my friend, Jim Martin. Jim dropped dead of a sudden heart attack at the age of 60. One minute he was working on a project in the barn, and the next, he was no more.

I had known Jim well for about two years, when he welcomed me as a fellow survivor in a cardiac rehab program. Two months earlier, I had had quintuple bypass surgery at 43 and was still in shock. The event was quite a surprise to me. I was with my wife in Peru on the first day of a vacation, when I started to get chest pains in a museum. I was laughing one minute about erotic pottery and the next clutching my chest in a bad impression of every TV death cliché known to man. I was told I was a very lucky man. "A day away from dead" was how the doctor phrased it.

Shortly after surgery, Jim came to visit. He was warm and encouraging, telling me he had had a heart attack at 40 but was going strong and that I too would soon be fine. This was hard to believe when I could barely walk two blocks without panting, let alone do the 150 sit-ups the class did every morning. But with a wink, he prodded me forward into a committed life of exercise and health. Soon I was feeling stronger and fitter than at any point in my adult life. The body is an amazing thing.

At Jim's service, I looked around at the many faces of my fellow cardiac mates. In the last six months, three from our ranks had died. The first, Buzz, died in his mid-50s while jogging. He was at the peak of fitness. We were stunned.

As a group of men, the cardiac group is not used to talking about feelings. Our support comes in our jokes and just plain being there in the morning. If you miss a week, you are bound to hear about it. That's just who we are.

Following Jim's service, I was talking with two of my mates, Mike and Barry. Our interaction was typical of who we are when we get together, no matter what the occasion.

"Hard, huh?" Barry said.

"Yeah," said Mike.

"Yeah," I chimed in. Long pause.

"Don't worry, Mike," I said. "You'll outlive us all."

"Probably piss on our graves. At least Dave's for sure," Barry rejoined.

"Drop dead, Barry," I joked.

"You first, Dave," he laughingly responded.

And so it went. There is no malice here. It is who we are when dealing with the closeness of death. For those of us who have been this close to becoming cosmic dust, there is a certain appreciation of the moment. We rarely talk about it, but it's in the eyes of dedication we each bring every morning to the gym. The way we push each other forward and tenderly ask about each other's health. We are reminded by our friend's death of the tentative nature of the moment. It is not just a Hallmark card to us. Jim's service was sadly once again a powerful reminder of that.

In the life of my fellow cardiac mates, we model this awareness through our view of life. Our behavioral action is twofold. First, we prepare for the long haul. We exercise and eat as if we are going to live for another 50 years. But in the same breath, we also know that at any moment, like Buzz or Jim, the rug could be pulled out. And when it's pulled out, it's pulled fast. Heart attacks are rarely slow affairs. Instead, the blackness comes quickly, with little or no opportunity to say your peace or make your closures. This leaves one with a deep appreciation of the day. And that, more than anything else, is what we will all tell you is the greatest gift in our disease. I still wake every morning, no matter where I am or how I feel, and gratefully think, Another day on the right side of the grass. It's a blessing.

For rehab patients, death's momentary appearance helps us solidify our health-style resolve. For instance, it would be foolish to forget our heart disease and live as if we have no problems. Big Macs are out for good. Yet, at the same time, we couldn't live every day worrying that this could be it and any moment our last. We'd be like scared rabbits in a wood filled with predators, shaking and tentative. What we intuitively do then is to prepare for both life and death.

This is the lesson of *full-powered presence*. It teaches us a balance between all-out attack and the willingness to let go entirely. This presence requires both simultaneous detachment and focus. Detachment means you are willing to release any hold you have over outcome. It implies that at a moment's notice you are willing to lay your life on the line. OK, maybe not your life, but your strategy, your action plan, or your position. Can you let go without fear or pride getting in the way and greet the day the way many Native American warriors greeted theirs: "It's a good day to die."

At the same time you release, however, you must also be ready to bring a warrior's spirit committed to full action. In aikido, this requires complete attention and bold response without hesitation. It is unequivocal and without doubt. It *goes* for it, plain and simple.

This delicate balance of emotional removal and simultaneous readiness for full-bore attack is not easy. But considered carefully, it makes sense. In battle, one who always only believes he or she can die at any moment will most likely create a self-fulfilling prophecy. Filled with resignation, he or she is an easy target. On the other hand, one who is constantly on the attack, flailing wildly with untamed aggression is also easy to defeat. He or she becomes weakened, unfocused, and at risk. The prudent course is then twofold: Stay open and detached to the possibility of loss, but simultaneously prepare for hard-fought gain.

This, in essence, is what my friends in cardiac rehab do. We prepare for the unpredictability of death by working hard at life-affirming behavior.

In the movie *Gladiator,* Russell Crowe, as the main character, opens the movie by running his hand over a field of grass before the key battle that will win the war. His way of preparing for the hugeness of his task is to stop and notice the small moments around him. By doing so, those moments give him the needed perspective and courage to mount his attack. This image, of trusting loss and gain as simultaneously essential, is what all great leaders have. It is what living in *full-powered presence* means.

TRY THIS . . .

- Put a small red sticky-dot on your watch.

- Every time you glance at your watch and see the dot, look around and remind yourself to stay fully present for one full minute.

- Ask yourself, "Am I balancing the two sides of presence?"

DB

STAY UNATTACHED TO OUTCOME

The past and the future are only sources for worry and anxiety.

—Zen proverb

After days of intense preparation, the merger team is ready for the 8 AM acquisition announcement the following morning. Presentations have been scripted, executives prepped, and a tight schedule of events coordinated across multiple locations to carefully communicate this important and controversial decision. After all, its employees have been living several months with the ambiguity of who will take over their company and ultimately, when the dust settles, whether they will have jobs.

At 7 PM, the buyer balks, delaying the final decision and requesting more customer data. The communications plan grinds to a sudden stop. Without skipping a beat, the merger team refocuses its activities. The team prepares a short statement, notifies all key executives, and prepares a briefing for managers. There is little time spent expressing frustration about the change, regretting the time and energy put into the announcement preparation, and being cynical about the potential buyer. The team responds with full energy and focus, quickly orienting to the next phase, as if the announcement was never a possibility. All in a day's work.

One of the *full-powered presence* tactics that the merger team used is called "staying unattached to outcome." According to Angeles Arrien, staying unattached to outcome is helpful in maintaining objectivity while accessing wisdom in any situation. From an aikido perspective, it means taking 100 percent committed action while simultaneously adjusting, if circumstances change. For a leader, it's the ability to thoroughly prepare for a project without assuming that events will occur in a certain way.

On the aikido mat, unattached to outcome is a helpful tactic to use. In a *randori* multiple-attack practice, you don't know which strike your opponents will offer, and though you have many techniques in your repertoire, you can't determine ahead of time which one you'll end up using. You're ready for anything. Trying to predict an attack—Joe really likes a double wrist grab, so I bet he's going to use that one—makes you twice as unprepared when Joe tries another strike. And just because you love *kaiten-nage,* a windmill throw, doesn't mean that will be the appropriate response to Joe's attack. There is a moment where you put aside all your knowledge of the technique and shift to letting the circumstances dictate your action.

In that moment, when you suspend your decisiveness and planning, you create an opening for more accurate assessment of the situation and effortless response. It's as if your system is poised, extensive energy coiled, and a full repertoire of responses ready for selection. Action is immediate and without delay, because you haven't prematurely gone down the wrong solution path. Resistance is nonexistent, because your response fits like a glove. The unattached-to-outcome process repeats itself continuously, restarting with each new attack. Unattached attitude—respond to the attack; unattached attitude—respond to attack.

When leaders are first introduced to this skill, they think they have to deliberately forget their knowledge, experience, and opinions about how to deal with a certain business problem. It feels like they are giving in or not being responsible as a leader by not planning ahead. Instead, after the usual problem assessment and planning, they try temporarily suspending their predictions about how a project should turn out and stay aware of how each phase is actually evolving. For example, rather than react to a colleague based on past history, be open to a different interaction each time.

The skill of being unattached to outcome complements the ability to be at *full-powered presence*. Locking into a certain way of doing things narrows your focus and constricts both your perspective and power. Unattached to outcome opens your perspective and expands your energy. Habitually using the same leadership approach creates resistance and struggle when it doesn't fit the person or situation. Unattached to outcome gives you the widest range of options to choose from, so your response tends to be more appropriate.

Unattached to outcome does not mean that you are so flexible that you never take decisive action. The two need to go hand in hand. Each of us has a propensity for being either too convergent or too divergent in our leadership approach. If you like to lock in decisions and are hesitant to change them down the road, you need to balance your leadership effectiveness with being more unattached to outcome. If you are keenly tuned in to the many changing variables in any given situation, it would be beneficial to emphasize putting the stake in the ground.

Full-powered presence teaches us that unattached to outcome is a skill that conserves vital energy by avoiding unproductive activity out of sync with what's needed. Moving on to the next scenario is quicker when there is no preconceived notion of what is supposed to happen. Resentment, skepticism, and regret are kept at a minimum when premature expectations are not allowed to overdevelop. Unattached to outcome combined with bold decisiveness leads to the path of effortless leadership.

TRY THIS . . .

- Identify an upcoming business decision.

- Write down your opinions about what you think should happen and why.

- Bring that piece of paper to the decision-making meeting but put it aside.

- Focus first on looking at the problem with a fresh perspective on alternatives.

- Only then advocate for your original opinion.

JH

TUNE INTO YOUR RADAR

Tell me what you pay attention to and I will tell you who you are.

—José Ortega y Gasset

When you are at *full-powered presence,* you have the opportunity to access information that can aid in your success. It makes sense that if you are calm, then you are able to efficiently process different alternatives, think "through" rather than hastily react, and sit with a decision to make sure it feels right. When you are centered, this discernment process doesn't necessarily take a lot of time. In a way, going slow first will enable you to go faster later. There's a quality of information processing that ensures making the right decision, one that can be boldly put into action.

However, there's another advantage found in the state of *full-powered presence*. You will notice that you can start to pick up information that is below the normal radar level where most people operate. These days, we are inundated with a constant avalanche of information and sensory stimulation. E-mail, voice mail, too many meetings, the ever-present TV screen, and the expectation that a message has to be entertaining in order to be received create information overload. For survival, most people screen out all information except the loudest or most important. They shut down their radar to try and cope.

When you are centered, focused, and at *full-powered presence*, you are able to acknowledge the information overload as background noise, just as you would if you got used to conducting business in a busy office space. The "noise" isn't a distraction that diminishes your performance. Without the need to close down the information flow, you can instead selectively tune into accessing more information, like a radar telescope pinpoints an area in space to listen to.

People communicate the most obvious information through the words they share.

The next level of information would include the emotions they express through voice, facial expression, and body language. On a more subtle level, people communicate their intentions about a project or another person through the energy they convey. If someone is skeptical about a project and is considering withdrawing, his energy will feel half-empty and tenuous. In contrast, a person who is excited and viewing a task or relationship as important will emit energy that is full and inclusive. Your radar will pick up energy that feels like a brick wall from someone who is resistant and may be secretly intending to sabotage a project.

Tuning your internal radar to a higher frequency so that you can pick up this subtle energy requires the following steps: First, you must take a moment to be centered, calm, relaxed and fully breathing, and free from pressing thoughts. Then, think about a person or a project and ask the question, "What else do I need to know about this person as we work together in this project?" Pay attention to any words, images, or energetic responses. If you don't receive anything, try it again later. Or pay attention to delayed messages. Consider the information as complementing what you already know, not necessarily as conclusive fact, although there are plenty of examples of subtle, energetic messages dramatically impacting the receiver for the better.

Here's an example: Bob managed a large technology change project, converting an entire manufacturing operation to a new inventory management system. He did his homework in terms of systems requirements, vendor selection, project planning, cost/benefit analysis, and supplier relationships. Any MBA faculty would consider his approach a textbook example of quality and thoroughness.

Bob also realized that to manage this project successfully, he needed to enlist the support of the operations managers, those who would be on the receiving side of the new system and ultimately make it work. He scheduled a meeting early on in the assessment phase to get their input and reactions. The meeting went well, with the usual mix of concerns and optimistic comments. Will the vendor be flexible and design a system that meets our needs? Does this mean we will be able to eliminate those five steps in our current process that never made any sense, were time consuming, and only seemed to benefit management? On the surface, Bob thought it was a good meeting, and he continued meeting with these managers throughout the design phase of the project.

Just before the final design decision point, where the operations managers would need to sign off on the plan, Bob decided to spend a minute "tuning his radar" more closely to this critical group. He wanted to check to see if there was more information available on a more subtle level. After taking a moment to get centered, he sat in his chair and, in his mind, called up an image of each operations manager. Bob then silently asked the question, What else should I know to make sure the project will be successful for everyone?

To a person, Bob experienced either neutral or positive energy when he focused on each manager, except when he thought of John, the most seasoned and respected veteran of the group. Bob knew that John was a man of few words, and having respectfully drawn him out in the meetings, thought John was on board. But this particular morning when Bob focused on John, he had an uneasy feeling and couldn't get a clear read like he could with the other managers. He didn't sense anything specific, no words of caution, just a "quality" that left him wondering how John really felt about the project.

Bob decided to trust his radar and went up to John's office. He acknowledged that John was crucial to the successful implementation of the new system and reiterated his commitment to customizing the technology to meet the department needs. He wanted to know if John had any additional thoughts that hadn't been voiced that he should know about. Then Bob sat back and listened. There was a long pause in the conversation. It was clear that John had more to say, and he was deciding whether he could trust Bob. Bob tried to stay centered, open-minded, and away from focusing on the impending implementation deadline.

Finally John spoke, relaying his concerns about the capabilities of two of the supervisors to make it in the new system, both of whom reported to his best friend. He didn't want to put his friend in the uncomfortable position of firing them. And then there were the extensive training requirements and his concern about meeting production targets. And, he didn't feel comfortable in the meeting relaying a confidential conversation he had had with a customer who had a less than satisfactory experience with the technology vendor. He had decided that he wasn't going to bring up these concerns and was hoping the worst scenarios wouldn't happen.

Needless to say, this was extremely helpful information for Bob to hear, and he found a way to tactfully make important changes to the project without breaching John's confidentiality. John became a strong supporter of the project and, given his reputation with the operations group, created a groundswell of enthusiasm. The project turned out to be a huge success.

Full-powered presence teaches us to pay attention to subtle, sometimes unseen messages. Tuning our radar to pick up words, emotions, facial or body expressions, and even the quality of energetic responses can be helpful in accomplishing projects or maintaining good working relationships. Pay attention to what your radar picks up and check out the messages. You may be pleasantly surprised.

TRY THIS . . .

- After a meeting, take a few minutes to document what you tracked about a colleague during the discussion.

- Note his opinions, emotional tone, level of physical energy, and any hunches you had about his participation.

- If the colleague is willing, share your perceptions to validate and fine-tune your radar and offer to do the same for him.

JH

THE TRAP OF INFLATION

Judgmental anger is like burning down
your own house to get rid of a rat.

—Japanese saying

Picture this: You've had a hard week. There has been a great deal of stress and pressure in your business. At three o'clock on Friday afternoon the week reaches a crescendo. During an all-staff meeting, it's revealed that your office in Ohio has been responding slowly on an IT issue. While not a crisis, it is a problem that must be dealt with quickly and effectively. But instead of managing the issue wisely, you hit the roof. Screaming and banging on the table, you take no prisoners. Your staff shrinks in fear. Rather than energized to respond, they leave the meeting with heads tucked down and demoralized. You're overreaction leaves you feeling frustrated and slightly embarrassed. There is little for anyone to feel good about.

Within all human interaction, there is a tendency to respond to stress and chaos by losing presence and inner balance. Among some traditional cultures, this loss of presence is referred to as "being out of one's hoop" or "soul loss." We know we are in this difficult place if one of two behaviors rises to the surface.

The first behavioral pattern is to move into a pattern of inflation. Angeles Arrien calls this "abnormalizing the normal." Essentially, this means we make mountains out of molehills. We take a relatively benign situation and blow it out of proportion. We rant, rave, foam at the mouth, and generally make a catastrophe out of the issue. Our fears run amuck, and our behaviors take off. We then start firing at any and all "attackers" in our general vicinity. And, this overreacting can be very damaging.

The rule of thumb to manage your way out of a chaotic mess is to "say what's so when it's so." This, of course, is not easy to do. But a few suggestions will help make you more effective in responding when out of your center.

When you find yourself making mountains out of mole-hills, try the following strategies suggested by Arrien.

First, speak only what is true for you without blame or judgment. Make sure you focus on the present, avoiding past or future generalizations, which are rarely helpful and often serve to only inflame a situation. Projecting blame or judgment makes the other party defensive and rarely creates a harmonious conclusion. So, stick to what sits in front of you and avoid dragging in unrelated feelings or concerns.

Second, watch any tendency to use absolutes: "We always" or "You never" or "Every single time." Psychologist Ann Repplier found that absolutes set up unnecessary resistance by creating immediate internal objections in the listener. Following an absolute, the listener will typically think, What do you mean I *never* keep you informed? Just last week I sent you an e-mail on our status. Jerk!

Whenever you hear absolutes creeping into your vocabulary, you know you are out of balance in your response.

A third consideration is to make sure your body language and tone reflect the level of the issue. If you have moved into inflation, tone and physical expression will usually mirror your feelings. You will get unnecessarily sharp, broad, or sarcastic. Watch your delivery method. If out of balance, this will be reflected in not just what you say but how you say it.

Finally, check your intention going into an issue. If you are heavily invested in "winning," you will have a tendency to cause harm. You need some time to slow down your thinking, so that you can be more effective. In this regard, use what the Japanese call "noble silence." *Noble silence* means we do not raise an issue until we know we can discuss it responsibly and without deep attachment to outcome.

In all matters of inflation, follow the wise words of theologian Thomas Aquinas, who said: "A trustworthy person is angry at the right person, for the right reason, at the right time, at the right level, in the right manner."

TRY THIS . . .

- Spend a week carefully tracking your tendency to inflate statements.

- Watch out for expressions that begin "You always" or "I never" or "This is the worst/best."

- Try making sure that everything you say is without exaggeration.

DB

THE TRAP OF DENIAL

I know nothing. I hear nothing. I see nothing.

—Sergeant Schultz in *Hogan's Heroes*

Scenario two: An unexpected issue has come up for your department. You are forced to make a complex and controversial decision that is somewhat time sensitive. Your current business environment is screaming at you to take action. If you choose one path, it's a substantial business risk and may ruffle some feathers. The other, safer path does nothing but reduce costs and offers far less upside return. Each choice has clear positives and minuses.

You delay action by setting up a task force to make recommendations, knowing full well its views will never be fully considered. You also keep putting the issue on meeting agendas but somehow never seem to get to it, choosing instead to place it on the back burner in favor of other less pressing concerns. When a team member raises the issue, you choose to bury any decision with a detailed request for more information. You hope and pray that the problem goes away before you have to deal with it and make a decision. You're feeling frozen and having trouble sleeping at night. It's a mess.

Sadly, you have fallen headfirst into the trap of denial and "out of your hoop."

The second response that tells us we are out of center, according to Arrien, is "normalizing the abnormal." To normalize the abnormal means we take difficult and challenging events and rather than deal with them straight-out, we pretend instead that everything is status quo. During denial, we frequently use the "F" word—fine—and plow ahead with our beliefs that conflict is the last thing we need.

The problem, of course, is that in our denial we can actually increase the potential for conflict later on. This is because of one clear and consistent thought, according to Arrien: The root of almost all conflict is either that we don't say what we mean or we don't do what we say. Denial is a way of not saying what we mean, and the impact can be as damaging as taking an inflammatory stance. It's just a bit more insidious.

If we remember that the path through chaos is to "say what's so when it's so," the following strategies will help if you find yourself in denial and out of your center.

First and foremost, *say it*. Take a breath, resist your fears and voice the issue. Oftentimes, we do not speak our peace because we fear we might be the only one who sees it that way. A rule of thumb in a team of eight to ten is: If one person has a feeling, at least two more will be feeling the same thing. Time and again, our experience has born out this rule of thumb. So, relax and say what's on your mind. You are probably not alone.

Second, because a change in communication behavior can be very stressful, it is helpful to rehearse in your mind what and how you will say what needs to be said. Remember, no one will typically make an effort to act on something he or she doesn't want to do in the first place. So, practice beforehand and in the moment of truth you will respond with less tension and effort.

Years ago, I went skydiving. I did it to get over my fear of heights. (Yes, I was scared, and no, it didn't work.) For an entire day, I practiced over and over three simple moves: arch, pull, and check. For literally six hours, I practiced the same three moves until I was sick of them. At the time, it seemed like overkill and frankly quite silly. However, when I was standing on the wing of the plane at 10,000 feet and thinking to myself, It's too late to go back in but I can't jump, my body *automatically* responded with arch, pull, and check. Even though my mind was on overload, my body flawlessly conducted a perfect jump. This fear, though more extreme, is not dissimilar to what people who use patterns of denial experience.

Finally, emotional tension over an unspoken issue must go somewhere. A frequent coping strategy for denial is to take the issue outside the appropriate circle. Rather than deal with the problem directly, we complain repeatedly *about* it to somebody else. This, of course, is potentially very hurtful. As a way of responding, I love the way the Inuit of the Canadian Arctic handle this pattern. They have a unique solution to avoid colluding in a harmful way.

If you go to an Inuit friend with a complaint, he will listen with patience and support three times to the same issue. But if you complain a fourth time, the listener will simply turn his or her back and walk away, because he believes you are more committed to the problem than seeking a successful resolution of the issue.

Try that one next time!

TRY THIS . . .

- Consider an opinion on an issue (it can be a small one) that you have left unsaid.

- Practice saying it without inflation or denial, but *say* it.

DB

AVOIDING THE TYRANNY
OF IMMEDIACY

Leaders must be close enough to relate to others,
but far enough ahead to motivate them.

—John Maxwell

Recently, I was on Wall Street in New York during the blowing in of Hurricane Floyd. It was something to behold. The city started to empty out at 1 PM. I never saw anything like it. By 3 PM, the entire financial district was empty. Of course, it ended up being no big deal. But the worry and fear propagated by the never-ending newscasts and Internet sites created an alarm among people rarely prone to overreaction. We are talking about New Yorkers here—and money people at that. Yet the number of phone calls made, the Web sites checked, and the frenzy created were impressive to witness.

Many I saw were calm, but many, a lot more than I would have thought, seemed to be in quite a state. It is a reflection, I believe, of the changing nature of information access and our response to that information.

Something has radically shifted in the world of organizational life with the advent of the Information Age. In years past, it seemed we were hungry for news and data. But today, the hunger seems more than interest or even passion. It seems addictive. The preponderance to sit hour-on-hour watching CNN or the Weather Channel rebroadcast the same news over and over is an ever-growing American trend. That addiction can bring with it a host of problems. With the acceleration of technology and information access, we are in jeopardy of being overwhelmed into poor discernment and overreaction. It makes it difficult to stay in *full-powered presence*.

A simple example is this: Just think how basic information *requests* have changed in the last decade. Ten years ago, if someone wanted you to have something quickly, they either overnight-mailed it or faxed it. The mode of transport used typically gave you time to sit and review the material with some sense of pacing. You could bring a quality of thoughtfulness to the process.

But with e-mail, entire documents are transported at the touch of a finger *and with it, a shifting expectation of response time*. More and more, my clients seem to be complaining they are becoming slaves to e-mail requests. They are coming in earlier and staying later just to catch up. Don't get me wrong. I love e-mail. I use it daily. It has made my life easier, and I definitely feel more connected around the world. I also believe a strong case can be made that the Internet is *the* technological breakthrough of the last 100 years.

But, it is not without its costs. (We have one client who gets 400–500 e-mails a *day*!) What is problematic is the inherent expectation that once a document is sent, a response is immediately forthcoming. The pressure mounts. It is a symptomatic issue reflective of a larger problem: our inability to separate the need for quiet thought from the influx of information and its resulting pressure. It is an issue in need of management.

The value of all this data is in its promotion of the growing process of data mining. The idea of "Let's see what we can find" is an ever-developing mindset among all types of people, with information access becoming *the* essential building block. When more and more people, with more and more access, can get almost all the information they want on any particular subject or area anytime they want—that's a lot of data potential.

The problem is, information is nothing more than that—*just data*. Data has no ascribed worth or value. The Internet does not sort the quality of material you receive. Late-breaking news is rarely discerning.

And when it comes to data assessment, it's important to remember that the process of data accumulation is different from the process of good judgment. They require different skill sets and different pacing. Data accumulation is speed and inductive based. Judgment takes wisdom, patience, and reduction. They are two very different breeds of cat—as different as the forest from the trees.

Because speed is often the driving force in most organizations, it must be tempered with an equal value placed on discernment.

This implies an important lesson: The expectation of increased response and information access warrants *more discernment and judgment than it ever has in human history.* Layer this with the trend to global connectivity—the idea that you may have work teams that *never* meet face-to-face— and the tendency to make more mistakes at a faster pace results in a complicated problem.

Full-powered presence teaches us that what's called for is a consistent return to remembering that data accumulation and its resultant speed are only one skill that needs to be rewarded and managed. There is another: a slower, more thoughtful process that is often forgotten in the haste of increasing pace. Good judgment can only come from giving oneself a lengthening of time. As information overload bears down on your day, ask yourself which of your issues requires real response. Which, if not addressed, will cause true damage, and which is nothing more than a whirling dervish of somebody's fear and can be dealt with in a more relaxed manner? The best executives we know find specific times every day to unplug themselves from the tyranny of immediacy and sink into a slower pace. Sometimes it's on a limo ride home, sometimes it's in the gym—but almost every leader we know does it as a *daily* ritual. They instinctively know one of the most important of the *randori principles:* Frenzy is rarely conducive for clearheaded action.

Sometimes the best thing you can do amidst chaos is to take a moment to breathe, assess the reality of the situation, and act from what you know to be true—not what you suspect or what your *reactions* are telling you must be done. If possible, create time every day away from the chaos to sort it all out. Find ways to separate the need for data accumulation from good discernment. Collect what must be collected, but never act from this alone. In important decisions, ask yourself: "What does my good judgment tell me to do?" Then act from that answer. It is the best way we know to avoid the addiction to instant information.

TRY THIS . . .

- Create one hour every day that is e-mail, beeper, and voice-mail free. Do not check or send e-mails during this time period.

- Each month add another hour till you have created an e-mail-free day.

- Or, continue with this practice until you can focus on a task for an hour without thinking about or checking external messages.

DB

A VICE-GRIP IS NOT YOUR ONLY TOOL IN LIFE

With every gust of wind
The butterfly changes its place
On the willow.

—Bashō

I admit that I was taking a break when they handed out the mechanical genes. My strategy for assembling toys at birthdays is to toss out the instructions, take a look at the beautiful example on the front of the box, and start putting together any combination of parts that looks like they should go together. I've come to assume that bolts will never come off if you strip the threads, manufacturers always give you

too many parts, and duct tape can fix anything that doesn't
look just right. I have also come to appreciate the simplicity
of my approach. You only need one tool, a Vice-Grip. Vice-
Grips are great because with brute force you can make any
two parts fit together. As tools go, Vice-Grips have a hefty
feel to them, which gives me an even greater sense of power.
Where would I be without them?

Typically in aikido, two people pair off, taking turns as
one person provides a certain attack. For example, one party
gets to provide a punch to the stomach area or a simulated
sword strike, while the partner practices the associated
aikido response. After a while, they switch roles. An attack
in aikido is provided with full power and clear intention—as
if it were a lethal strike. A halfhearted attack means you are
unnecessarily taking care of your practice partner. In reality,
people rarely get hurt. It is their intent of attack that is most
important.

In my study of aikido, it became apparent that I had
transferred my love of Vice-Grips to other parts of my life.
My aikido teachers, Chris Thorsen, Richard Moon, and Steve
Kalil, as well as my very helpful practice partner, Michael,
were quick to point out the force and rigidity of my attacks.
For a while, they even nicknamed me after my favorite tool.

The way I translated "attacks of high integrity" was to
move into Vice-Grip-like rigidity. If the attack required me to
grab someone's wrist to prevent her from getting away, I'd
clamp on with all my strength and lock my muscles. I thought
that if I were really forceful, I would give my partner a challenging attack and a worthy practice opportunity. I particu-

larly enjoyed being called up by one of my teachers to help demonstrate the next aikido technique. My six-foot, one-inch height and grimacing facial expression provided a perfect demonstration for how to deal with a forceful attack.

What was perplexing was that the more forceful my attack, the harder my fall to the practice mat. I thought I was making it more difficult for them to respond, when in fact, I made it easier. The stronger my grip, the easier it was for them to escape.

Here's why: In order to be forceful, I had to adopt a rigid stance, and when someone is rigid, he is surprisingly easy to move. When I only focused on tightening my grip, I got tunnel vision and couldn't effectively react to my partner's response. It was clear that I was physically off balance, and if my partner stepped to either side, it didn't take much energy on her part to redirect my attack. Finally, by locking up all my energy in one attack, it was hard to defend myself on the next one. The consequence was that I left myself wide open to some hard falls.

After taking dozens of jarring trips to the mat, it began to sink in that my Vice-Grip attack strategy had some flaws. My teachers posed the question, "How could I provide a full-powered attack without losing my balance or perspective and still have the flexibility to respond?" Initially, it was confusing. It felt like all I had was an on/off switch, either Vice-Grip or namby-pamby. Namby-pamby described low energy and minimal effort. This created two things. First, it left my partner feeling I wasn't giving her a substantial attack to work with. Worse, I felt like a pushover. Later I learned that sometimes on the learning curve we do the opposite of what we know, as a step to discovering the alternatives in between.

Over time and with helpful guidance, I found the balance point where I could provide an attack with high energy and clear intention but with the adaptability to instantly respond to my partner's counterattack. As a consequence, my attack became continual, providing a solid foundation for my partner's response. There was no question in my partners' minds that if they didn't respond well my attack would find its mark. I was giving them plenty of power to work with. But because I was also focused on being flexible in my response, my falls became more graceful, and even exhilarating. When I didn't revert to my Vice-Grip approach, there was no resistance for my partner to deal with. Instead of a power struggle, we were able to create a dynamic, creative exchange of energy.

Early in my business career, I managed a team of management trainers and organization consultants for a Fortune 500 company. Even though I had a capable team, I got overinvolved in the detail of each person's projects. I had a hands-on management style and liked to troubleshoot client crises. Requiring frequent meetings with my direct reports, I believed I was keeping informed. I wanted to be able to answer any question my boss had about our operation, at any moment. What I didn't realize was that I was stifling my colleagues with my overattention to detail and overinvolvement in their projects. They felt I was too controlling and undermined their initiative to lead a project. I thought I was being helpful. My team felt pinched by my Vice-Grip style of management. By backing off, I was surprised that results actually increased, my direct reports were happier, and I had extra energy to focus on higher-level projects.

Full-powered presence teaches us to pay attention to our approach when trying to accomplish a task or work with another person. It is possible to try too hard or be too forceful in fulfilling our expectations. Becoming rigid and forceful creates resistance and, ultimately, a power struggle. Adopting a dual attitude of clear intention with flexibility of response lays the groundwork for a productive relationship and high-energy results.

TRY THIS . . .

- Ask your direct reports or peers if you seem to be overcontrolling or overinvolved in any projects that they are leading.

- Invite them to be specific in their feedback.

- Consider other alternatives to support their success.

JH

TRUISMS ARE NOT TRUTH

The map is not the territory.

—Unknown

There is a story told about a man who saves his money to buy a handmade suit from the finest tailor on Saville Row in London. After being measured for two solid hours, the famous tailor tells him to return in two months. When he excitedly returns and tries his suit on for the first time, he's surprised to find it doesn't remotely come close to fitting. The left leg is four inches too long. The right sleeve is three inches too short. The seat is baggy, and the crotch is crooked and dimpled. "This suit doesn't fit," the man cries in exasperation. "You're wrong," says the tailor. "It's perfect. You're just not wearing it right." "What do you mean?" says the man. "Well," says the tailor, "take your left hand and pull up on your pant leg. Good. Now take your right hand and pull out your crotch. Great. Now hunch your right shoulder, jut your chin forward, slide your left leg forward, and push your pelvis back. Perfect!" The man leaves the store limping and contorting his way down the street. A few blocks later he passes two men at a bus stop. "My God," one says. "Will you look at that poor man? How in the world do you imagine he got so disfigured?" "I don't know," says the other. "But where do you think he got that *great fitting suit?*"

This is a terrific teaching story. It helps us see the difference between what we know to be true and what others tell us.

Recently, I had a conversation with my friend Roger Low, the managing partner of The Parallax Fund, a successful investment group. Roger says the primary challenge he faces in his job is to separate truisms from truth. He defines *truisms* as the common wisdom propelled forward by mass momentum. *Truth* on the other hand is what he knows deep down to be bedrock and unshakable. For instance, the market is filled with truisms about growth and/or decline, some driven by exuberance, some by rumor, some by pessimism, and little based on actual truth.

Full-powered presence teaches us to do our best to ignore truisms and focus instead on truth. This, of course, is easier said than done. Finding truth is not a science. It may not even be an art. It means returning to your internal compass when you are in need of guidance. Roger Low says it wonderfully: "To what degree I pay attention to what's going on outside of me and don't pay attention to what's happening inside of me, I'm in trouble."

In any tough and challenging situation, we will be tested to define the common wisdom of the day by the voices of others all around us, some of them "experts." We know we are in chaos when those voices seem to be either in conflict with each other or with our natural instincts.

Full-powered presence respects above all else the internal voice and guiding principles that we build our foundations on. O'Sensei, the founder of aikido, had as his foundation a combination of Shinto, martial arts, and the natural world. His critical actions and decisions ran through the screen of these internal compass points. Likewise, it is critical for you to know and act from your core beliefs, because by acting from your truths, you can decide quickly in the middle of chaos or attack.

Imagine you are on a mat, and you've got a guy running at you with the full intention of putting his fist through your stomach lining. The commitment of his attack and the lack of time do not allow for a wavering response. He charges you this hard, because without the full commitment of his assault, you both know you might be able to bullshit your way out of it. His intensity is, in fact, a form of honor and support (something to think about the next time you are getting grilled in a meeting). He attacks this way to hold you to the highest standard.

You only have time to respond effectively in one manner—with your core strategy. All other actions will prove painful. This is the time you must quickly pare down to what is most important and respond *only from that place*. As you go inward, your core beliefs tell you, "Do no harm, act from center, move *with* the force, stay connected to the attacker." As he engages, you focus on these principles and your intentions create the physical action. You sidestep and allow the attack to pass, as you grab an arm and throw your opponent to the mat unharmed. Your truths have provided the pathway.

For my friend Roger, his core truths drive his action: "family above all," "honest fairness to everyone I work with," "patience in making profit," "truth-telling in conflict," and "making a positive difference." As he rides the roller coaster of the market, these five truths guide his every decision. The more complicated the issue, the more he returns to match any potential action against the bellwether of his beliefs. And, he has been very successful sticking to what is for him truth.

In complex times, it is almost always simple and clear actions that get us through. But simple does not mean easy. The common wisdom of the day, the critical mass of truism, may be telling you something other than what you *know* to be true for you. When pressured by competing forces, take a deep breath and ask yourself, "What is my truth on this issue?" It may be a personal value, a business desire, a perspective on the customer, or a view of a balanced work and personal life. It will be different for every individual. But your truths will hold from situation to situation. They will seem right, even when inconvenient or unpopular. Sometimes finding our truths is a lifelong challenge. But when we do, if we hold them forward with courage and commitment, we will never be let down. The path will always be clear.

TRY THIS . . .

- Create a list of your five to ten great personal truths.

- Then, ask yourself how often are these truths supported in your work and personal life?

DB

THE POWER OF RITUAL

Ritual is the way we stay honest with the universe.

—Sobonfu Some

You are about to be tested for your third-degree Black Belt. You've worked hard for ten years to get to this place in your training. Before the "test," you start to get ready. It starts with putting on your *gi*, the practice uniform, and in particular, the specific way that you tie your belt. For you, feeling the belt knot pressing against your stomach reminds you to stay centered. Taking a moment to acknowledge O'Sensei reminds you of the thousands of aikidoists who came before you and the thousands who will follow. Connection to this bigger picture helps you become less anxious.

You take one step onto the actual mat, respectfully bowing to the picture of the founder, and then sit. You focus your mind by breathing deeply and with intention. Finally, the test begins and your partner approaches. You deeply bow to your opponent. This bow is more than a sign of deep respect. It is also a trigger to your mind—one that links you to all of the techniques learned over the years and the larger dance of aikido. In one singular movement the bow says that it's show time. Your body responds as you move into effortless action. Amazingly, the most seasoned aikidoists in the room knew you would be successful before the test began. How? Your ritual preparation told them so.

Dr. Jim Loehr and Peter McGlophlin, in their landmark book, *Mental Tough,* described the value of ritual for performance. In their research, Loehr and McGlophlin found that among professional athletes mental change was usually instigated by physical behavior. If an athlete wanted to change his mental state during competition, he first had to generate some kind of specific movement—do something in action with the body before the mind felt the impact.

Loehr and McGlophlin believe that changing the body will change the mind. This is an interesting premise, because it runs contrary to most conventional thinking that the mind controls the body. But, they contend, the opposite is true. For instance, they say, watch a professional tennis match. Observe during critical points, when the keenest of focused thought is required, how often Pete Sampras will straighten his racquet strings. Or before serving a big point, how many times Jimmy Connors will bounce a tennis ball. With Connors, the bigger the point, the more bounces. Both players created a physical action or ritual to change an inner mental state.

Another example: It is well known among experts that if you want to relieve depression, take up running. Running releases chemicals in the blood that increase energy and a sense of well-being in the individual. A depressed person can use physical activity as a powerful method for calming the mind and creating emotional change.

Still in doubt? Try this basic action the next time you need to feel more confident in a given situation. Extend your stride by six inches when you walk. That's all. Notice the difference you feel internally and the outward manifestations of how others see you. Most people who act more confidently in their walk will look and feel more confident in their manner.

This powerful example works, because you are creating a physical activity or ritual that supports the leadership qualities you want to show. The lesson is clear: Start first with the body to impact the mind.

Anything physical will also help "shift" a pattern. An activity or change of venue can be very successful at shaking you or others from a position. Jim and I are in the habit of either going for a walk to work out issues or practicing our swordplay (to be truthful, he teaches and I bumble). In Japan, the traditional way to deal with depression is through hard physical labor. It is a way to physically shift the environ-

ment and allow for a return to presence. By changing an outward manifestation, we can help change an inner sense of self.

I have a client who, before every big meeting, takes five
minutes to prepare himself with a wonderful ritual. He does
the following: He first walks around his office, so he gets his
energy moving. Then, he stops in front of a picture of his
family and says out loud, "Remember what is most important." He actually talks to himself. Once he is sure that the
ritual has taken hold, he then acts from that value. If you ask
people who work for him why he is so successful, they will
say things like, "He supports me at work and at home" or "I
always feel like he is operating out of a deep sense of values."
No one in his company knows he does this. In fact, he would
be embarrassed if people found out. But in difficult negoti-
ations, he is well regarded for his ability to go right to the
heart of an issue—a skill he reinforces through ritual almost
daily by remembering his family as his short list.

Full-powered presence teaches us that if we want to think
or behave in a certain manner, it is helpful to create rituals in
our bodies to support that thinking. If you want to be more
focused, create focusing rituals. If you want to be more
assertive, walk or prepare in an assertive fashion. If you want
to be ready for battle, create a process that will get your mind
and body ready for the attack. To translate the analogy to
effortless leadership: If you want to feel more effective, you
must first start to act more effectively. And, creating rituals
before you must actually perform can help prepare you for
this transition.

TRY THIS . . .

- Keep a picture of your family or a close friend in your office. Before every big meeting, take one minute to look at it (make it a full minute) and remind yourself what's really important.

- Create a similar ritual with your team.

DB

HELP OTHERS TO GET BACK INTO PRESENCE

If you can smile when things go wrong,
then you have someone in mind to blame.

—Unknown

Recently, I was the keynote speaker to a group composed of 150 CEOs of major companies in the Philadelphia, New Jersey, and Delaware market. Whenever I get the chance to speak in front of 150 decision makers in my business, that's a big deal. About 15 minutes before my presentation, I decided to follow some advice I had heard years ago regarding public speaking, which to this day has served me well: "Always, always, ALWAYS go to the rest room before you speak!"

I was speaking at the Four Seasons Hotel in Philadelphia, an establishment of the highest quality. I was a little nervous as I headed down the hall, thinking of my talk. That's where my problem started! These days, in many hotels, rather than spell out the word *Men,* an international sign of a man or woman is used instead. With my mind on the upcoming presentation, I proceeded to push open the bathroom door I thought was for men.

My first thought as I looked up was, That's funny, there are no urinals in here. Must be a *European* men's room.

Then I looked to my left and saw 15 to 20 women standing at a mirror, pointing and laughing. Now I may have a Ph.D., but I want to tell you, I'm not always the brightest light on the street. So, I glanced at these women and thought, That's funny, what are all these women doing in the *men's room?*

Fortunately, at that point I realized the error of my ways and darkness descended! I don't know if you've ever walked into the wrong rest room, but it is a horrifying experience. Bells, whistles, and sirens all went off in my head.

It was then my mind switched into overdrive: Quick, think fast. In my mind's eye, I saw myself turning to these women and saying in a smooth voice, "Pardon me, ladies, I seem to have the wrong facility." Then leaving with grace and aplomb.

That was the plan. Unfortunately, when the words hit my mouth and left my lips, it sounded like, "Uhhh, Uhhhh, Arghhh, OH MY GOD!" I then ran out of the women's room and right into the woman who had hired me to give the talk in the first place!

I was speechless and visibly shaken. But worse, I had been "caught" by my client. As a consequence, I was having a hard time concentrating on my talk. I was not, as they say, "on." I couldn't concentrate on the job at hand. All I could think about was the embarrassment of getting caught.

My client, a terrific woman, sensed my anxiety and helped me to view the situation through *full-powered presence*. After reading my biography to the group, she concluded her opening remarks by saying, "And now, a man who for *many* of you needs no introduction!" As I laughingly approached the podium, she whispered, "Relax, it will make a great story for a book." I never looked back. The talk went splendidly.

This is a great example of helping someone else get back into his or her presence. In your job as a leader, it is sometimes critical to help others act to the best of their own potential. Fear, anxiety, frenzy, and embarrassment are just a few of the ways you can remove yourself from center. The list is as long as the variations of human behavior. But as a leader, there are a few things you can do regardless of these differences that will bring your people back to their finest.

In our experience, there are three primary ways to assist. While not the full complement of actions you can take, they represent a large percentage of responses that can prove useful.

Strategy number one, surprisingly, is to do nothing. Sometimes, action is the last thing an individual needs. Silence, quiet support, and avoiding increasing the frenzy are surprisingly effective choices. They are especially effective when your employee is so wound up that any comments you offer only create additional concern. If this is the case, then quietly breathe and allow time to slowly bring her back to "home base." Use time well. Then, when the moment is right, reassure and move forward as if everything is perfect. This space and encouragement will allow your colleague to naturally shift back to center.

Another main strategy is to provide information and/or on-the-spot coaching for the individual in difficulty. Sometimes, individuals get off center because they are struggling to be effective with a lack of knowledge and skill. In this case, providing instant informational support can give the confidence needed to move forward. Ask yourself, "Is there information my employee currently doesn't have that if available would decrease her anxiety?" This may require spending a few moments considering any possible gaps in the employee's knowledge or skill base. Once identified, quickly and with assurance provide it.

A third and final option is to judiciously use humor. This is what my client did. Through her judicious and supportive wit, she helped break my internal ice, get me to laugh at my worst fears, and help me to move to a more relaxed place. She didn't belabor the point or make herself the center of attention. Instead, quickly and with focus she shifted my anxiety into laughter.

The value of humor is that it can help break the tension of the moment and move us away from our attachments. Often, the attachment is to look good or be in perfect control. When we laugh, especially if the humor is well intended, it helps loosen our self-image grip—and that aids relaxation, confidence, and self-assurance.

Imagine this: Make a fist and hold it tight. Now, have a friend try to force your fist open in an aggressive manner. What is your reaction? You fight back and resist. Your fist remains shut despite your friend's best efforts. Force of will creates unnecessary resistance. You struggle and remain in your pattern.

Now, make another fist and this time have your same friend laughingly, slowly, and gently pull each finger apart. Notice how your hand opens like a flower blooming in the spring. What a difference! This is what well-timed humor does to return a colleague to center.

But, to be successful means more than just using the right technique. You also must deliver it in the right way. *Full-powered presence* teaches us that to be effective requires two delivery skills. The first is to make sure the action we take matches the needs and personality of the individual. Humor worked well with me. With another person, in another situation, it may be less effective, so pick your encounter carefully. Remember, your colleague is not at his or her best and so may be prone to either overreaction or denial. An effortless strategy is one that matches not just the situation but also the personality.

The second delivery skill is to do everything possible in this action to allow your colleague to save face. A loss of face will only make an already difficult situation worse and will take him or her further from his or her natural center. Imagine if I had been overly teased by my client and lost face in front of my audience.

If you start to become attentive to your relationship environment, you will soon become sensitive to when others are lacking in presence. Angeles Arrien says that the "weakest link on any team are those who are not participating. And that is defined by those not emotionally or intellectually present." Look for these links and then do what you can to bring others back to presence.

TRY THIS . . .

- Actively spend one month looking for colleagues who are not at full presence.

- During meetings, work sessions, or giving presentations, track why they are not present and what you need to do to bring them back.

DB

TENKAN

TURNING
RESISTANCE
INTO
COLLABORATION

WHAT IS TENKAN?

There should be less talk.
A preaching point is not a meeting point.

—Mother Teresa

There are no offensive attack techniques in aikido. Punches and strikes are only provided to help aikidoists practice defensive responses. In the spirit of aikido, when you find yourself wanting to attack someone, it is an indication that you are out of balance with yourself; you are operating out of disrespect and mistrust; and you are out of sync with your team, organization, and as O'Sensei would say, "the universe." Aikido's defensive techniques are geared towards helping an attacker reconsider his intentions and return to balance. At the master level, the harder the attack, the more graceful the response, so that with a few small movements, the sensei will neutralize a strike without even touching the attacker. It seems like magic.

It is also known in the aikido world that linear and oppositional interactions tend to escalate conflict rather than resolve it. In that spirit, many aikido techniques are circular and focus on redirecting the force of an attack and not on stopping or overpowering it. By getting closer to your opponent, you can sense his next attack before it takes place. If an attack is neutralized before it gains full power, it is easy to redirect. Over time, a person who keeps attacking gives up or gets exhausted, never getting the satisfaction of a strike hitting its mark. If attacks are handled in such a way that your opponent is not humiliated or embarrassed, he will transform the initial aggression to one of high respect. The "victim" is now seen as a worthy adversary, thus giving the attacker a chance to honorably change his ways and save face.

Tenkan is the aikido tactic where you get off the line of the strike and move closer to your attacker in order to dissipate the energy of his attack. Circular in nature, *tenkan* combines grace and power to neutralize attacks. A punch or strike seems to evaporate with no target to hit, and the attacker, now completely off balance and no longer having the will or energy to attack, safely falls to the mat. It is in part due to the spiral nature of *tenkan* that aikido is called the dance of the martial arts.

Off the mat and in the business world, *tenkan* is a valuable skill for a leader. By quickly neutralizing opposition and dissipating resistance to an idea, leaders can more effectively implement critical business initiatives. *Tenkan* creates a base for creative problem solving and an environment for collaboration, not destructive conflict.

For example, many times business colleagues may lash out, using too much aggression to make a point or for a moment losing sight of the value of mutual respect. In other situations, direct reports may have a high level of anxiety in times of major change, attributing to hesitancy or resistance. Other colleagues come on too strong, either because that's their personality or because they are trying to force an opinion on others. These behaviors get in the way of effective teamwork and accomplishing business goals. Leaders need to quickly and effectively address these situations before they derail projects or develop into a dysfunctional organizational dynamic.

Tenkan in the business world emphasizes the following four tactics:

1. Pay close attention to your colleagues or adversaries. Listen carefully to what they have to say. Can you paraphrase their main message? Have they built up a head of steam about their opinion or are they tentative? What is the timing of the issue? Is it something that has been recently triggered or has it been brewing for a long time? Find as many ways as possible to get close to your people and their issues.

2. In order to do this, you have to temporarily suspend your own opinions about the situation or your responses to your colleagues' position. You aren't agreeing but placing a priority on understanding their perspective over trying to persuade. That comes later. By suspending your opinion, you limit the chances of creating an oppositional argument. Without opposition, the situation can't escalate into entrenched conflict. Ultimately, you adopt the attitude of being willing to be moved or persuaded by your colleague.

3. Listen until their emotions, enthusiasm, or self-righteous opinions subside. *Tenkan* goes beyond reflective listening and pays attention to not only the message but also the emotion and energy behind it. Keep asking about their position until they are calm or have nothing to say. Be careful not to use your questions as

attacks ("Could you describe your ridiculous idea for me one more time?") or to buy time to prepare your rebuttal. Your colleagues will know whether you are genuinely interested and when you are playing games.

4. When people feel heard, they are more open to listening to other perspectives. If they have had a chance to express their emotions and energy, they will more easily consider other alternatives. For example, someone who comes on strong may need a chance to talk through his passionate ideas and retell his story a few times before being willing to engage in a two-way conversation.

Tenkan creates common ground where the highest level of creativity and collaboration can occur. When faced with aggressive or resistant colleagues, first make sure you are at *full-powered presence*. Then choose to find a way to get close to your "attacker." Your goal is to truly understand his view, while providing a chance to dissipate any aggressive energy. You're not giving in or being overly accommodating to demands. Instead, with *tenkan,* you are minimizing the chances of conflict escalation, while advocating for the best mutual decision with the least struggle and effort.

JH

GET OFF THE FIRING LINE

Between what I think I want to say, what I believe
I'm saying, what I say, what you want to hear, what
you believe you understand, and what you understood,
there are at least nine possibilities for misunderstanding.

—François Garagnon

You probably know the feeling. That uneasy sense your boss is targeting you for reprimand or accusation. You may even get an early warning signal of some sort, like in the movie *Top Gun,* when the cockpit alarm sounds that the enemy has a missile locked onto your plane. Your skin begins to crawl. You may even begin to squirm in your seat, while checking for the nearest exit. If the attack happens in a team meeting, you can almost hear the collective sigh of dread, as your colleagues seem to whisper, "Poor bastard, hope he survives this one."

Unfortunately, there are still leaders in the corporate world who think that, because of their position or title, they are entitled to unlimited power. They will try to use fear and public embarrassment as motivation tactics, underestimating the distrust and resistance their actions will breed. These ineffective managers forget that sensitive issues should be dealt with off-line, in private, so that a colleague maintains self-esteem in the eyes of her peers. These leaders are often clueless to the impact of a fierce, disrespectful public attack. They are typically naïve to the fact that the story will quickly spread through the organization, thus severely handicapping their chance of building future allegiances. Occasionally, an executive knows all this and just doesn't care what harm she inflicts. Those executives are the most dangerous ones.

A typical reaction to a surprise attack is to freeze up. Without a prepared response and fearing escalation, most people stay quiet, hoping that if they don't respond the attack will end quickly. The other typical pattern of response is to accommodate the attacker by agreeing with whatever she says, hoping she will back off.

Unfortunately, neither of these tactics works. Freezing up or appeasement drains your energy. And when your energy goes minus, you actually invite more attack energy to fill the void. These approaches label you as a target in the future, and the more often this dynamic occurs, the more indiscriminate and disrespectful the accusations become. What may feel like momentary relief actually encourages more frequent difficulty.

The opposite approach, full-out counterattack, doesn't work much better. Disrespectful aggression, fueled by both parties, tends to escalate the conflict, and eventually someone loses. If it's your boss you are locking horns with, that someone who loses will be you. You don't want to add fuel to the fire when your boss is off center. Publicly arguing with a superior can have long-term negative consequences. It may feel good in the moment to push back, and you may even get encouragement from your teammates for your challenge, but eventually you will end up like Joan of Arc.

If neither denial nor force is effective, what is the alternative to dealing with an aggressive attack? The key is to get off the line of the attack.

In aikido, the first response to an incoming attack is to get off the line or move your body out of the way of the punch or strike. Watching the punch miss your body and slide past you allows you to maintain a calm perspective, since you are now out of the target zone. Once off the line, you can move closer to your opponent and neutralize future attacks. Without any gratification of hitting their target, eventually opponents either exhaust themselves or shift their intention to a more collaborative one.

In the workplace, getting off the line first requires that you be aware of your boss or colleague shifting to a more aggressive tone rather than a respectful, candid, and collaborative one. If this is the case, your first step is to make sure you are at *full-powered presence,* so that your energy doesn't go "minus," encouraging more aggressive intensity. From this vantage point, you can view the attacks without taking them personally and with a little distance.

Once off the line, you can try to understand the rationale of her attacks while dissipating the force. This is different from asking questions in order to prepare a counterattack. If you're out of the target zone, you can give your boss the opportunity to return to a more respectful business discussion and salvage a reputation that may be on the line.

Here's an example: Rich is sitting in a quarterly business review meeting with his boss, the CEO, and his colleagues. Out of the blue, his boss starts attacking him for the lack of new product success in the Northeast region. Feeling on the spot and knowing his usual tendency is to immediately attack back, Rich senses that his boss is more stressed out and less objective than normal. He chooses to focus on his own breathing rather than on becoming tense. From this place, he prepares his response. Calmly listening while his boss openly criticizes his operation is tough, but it gives him some clues that he does not have all the facts.

"Bill, you have every right to be frustrated," Rich calmly started. "I would be, too, if I had drawn the same conclusions from the data you cited. I know we are under a lot of pressure this quarter, and my commitment to our success has not wavered. Can we take each data point and talk about the implications?"

The CEO paused for a second and then launched into another attack, this time with less aggression. Each time, Rich was calm and respectfully careful not to embarrass his boss. And each time, he added some new data and his perspective to the discussion. Using phrases with a calm demeanor, like "Bill, I want to understand your perspective" and "I welcome any suggestions from you or anybody else on the team," Rich gradually addressed Bill's concerns without escalating the attacks. Even though he never agreed with Bill's opinions and it was clear his boss had significant gaps in information, Rich successfully derailed his boss's attacks and redirected the conversation to a more productive team discussion about future market trends. Stepping off the line of Bill's attacks was crucial.

A simpler action to getting off the firing line is to position yourself to the *side* of an antagonist at a meeting table, so that you are not in the line of sight. Here, you literally get off the firing sight line. Those in front of an angry bull are the ones who will usually get gored. Those who strategically place themselves out of view are more easily able to either avoid trouble or engage in *tenkan* response without bearing the full brunt of an angry attack.

Tenkan teaches us that the first move of response to attack is to step off the line. From that vantage point, we can remain calm and keep a broad perspective of the situation. In this case, by getting some distance and not taking Bill's attack personally, Rich was able to see that his boss was lacking information. To aggressively counterattack and point this out would have caused Bill embarrassment and escalated the conflict to a no-win contest. It took three rounds of listening to his boss's concerns and carefully adding missing information before Rich felt that Bill was able to discuss the business issue from a knowledgable and nonreactive state. Once off the line, we more effectively get at the heart of a business issue. This is what *tenkan* is all about.

TRY THIS . . .

- In a heated discussion, avoid taking an oppositional stance and overpersonalizing another's comments.

- Instead, picture yourself outside the target zone of their attacks, and from that off the line position diffuse the conflict.

JH

GET CLOSE TO
YOUR ATTACKER

Keep your mind like the vast sky,
the highest peak, and the deepest ocean.

—O'Sensei

Many of the aikido responses to an attack are circular in form rather than linear. Relying on only linear techniques increases the chances that the conflict will escalate because of oppositional positioning. One of the benefits of choosing a circular path is that it allows us to see many perspectives on an issue rather than just one. It also gives us a chance to get closer to our attacker.

Ironically, one of the safest places to be when under verbal assault is close to your attacker. You can sense the degree of power behind the attack, the degree of balance the attacker has, and the welling up of his next assault. You can convey a calm and centered tone and more directly communicate your clear intentions when you are in contact with your adversaries. The message they receive is that you want a peaceful resolution of the conflict but won't be a victim. By anticipating their next move, you can neutralize their attack before it gains power. When several of their antagonistic attacks are futile and you provide no resistance for their reaction, opponents will either shift to a more collaborative stance or move onto another potential victim.

Here's an example: Janet is about to present to a room full of sales managers. She relies on them to distribute her new line of products, so the stakes are high. When a new line comes out, the sales managers are naturally skeptical and, in a large meeting presentation, will typically test Janet's market research and new product rationale. They are piranhas, poised to rip apart any presentation at the first hint of weakness.

Janet has done her homework and knows the details of the presentation well. Before the meeting starts, she does a visual scan of the audience, remembering key managers who can make or break her pitch. There's Hugo, who will first appear to endorse the new line but may suddenly drill her for merchandizing ideas. Mary will come on strong from the start, focusing on the market demographics. On the other hand, Juan, the most respected and senior of the managers, won't comment but will instead convey influence through his body posture. Arms crossed signals disapproval; arms open and leaning forward means he likes what he is hearing.

Janet knows that if she overly focuses on these key managers or gets too wrapped up in her own presentation, she will not be successful. A concise, hard-hitting, inspiring presentation is important, but not if she loses awareness of her audience. She knows she will be more vulnerable if she doesn't pay attention.

Janet prepares by first relaxing and taking a few deep breaths. Doing so allows her to take in the people congregating in the room. She makes a special effort to visually connect to each person as they arrive, as if she is greeting them with a silent handshake. Time slows down a bit, and people start easing into their chairs. Janet's goal is to maintain awareness of each sales manager while delivering her presentation.

Not two minutes into the presentation, Mary, already attacking the timing of the new product launch, interrupts Janet. Maintaining her composure, Janet is careful to understand the nature of dissension without getting defensive or annoyed about the interruption. It turns out that Mary had some inaccurate information about a competitor's new line. Janet takes a moment and then proceeds.

A few minutes later, Hugo jumps in with a question. This time Janet finds herself suddenly looking at one side of the room, just as he fires off his unannounced concern from that same direction. It's almost as if Janet senses the buildup of energy as Hugo is formulating his attack. This sequence repeats itself several times during the presentation. If she can maintain her awareness of and connection with her managers, then they will almost signal to her when they are going to challenge her ideas. The moment she gets defensive or too focused on finishing her talk, the frequency of attacks goes up and Janet appears more vulnerable. By remembering that she doesn't have to match the aggressive nature of her audience, she can remain calm and answer their questions in a nondefensive way.

Afterwards, it's clear that the meeting has been a success. The sales managers express their approval of the new product line and launch plan. Juan confides in Janet afterwards that it isn't the product line itself that most impresses him. It's Janet's ability to calmly handle tough questions that gives him confidence the line will be a success.

Tenkan teaches us to get close to our adversaries in conflict. Getting and keeping them on our radar screen is a success factor in a relationship. Really taking the time to understand their viewpoint doesn't mean that we have to agree. When people feel acknowledged and heard, their oppositional energy subsides. Only myopically focusing on the task at hand leaves us vulnerable to unexpected attack. We gain the confidence of others not only in what answer we give but also the tone in which we respond. The lesson is to stay calm and get close to our attackers.

TRY THIS . . .

- Get close to an aggressive colleague by listening to him and confirming your understanding of his opinions, until emotions have dissipated and the colleague is open to collaboration.

JH

JOIN WITH YOUR ADVERSARY

The greatest motivational act one can do for another is to listen.

—Roy Moody

Consider the following scenario: You are running a challenging meeting. In the room sits a highly resistant individual who is more than willing to act out his concerns. At some point during the session, this individual raises his hand and when called on shoots a heat-seeking missile in your direction. Typically, it sounds like this: "I've got some *serious* problems with what you are proposing. In fact, I think it's absurd!"

All eyes focus on him and then back in your direction. Everyone wants to know what you are going to do. It's a challenge, a gauntlet thrown, and it is now time to respond.

Most leaders will typically act in one of two ways. The first common strategy will be to return fire with an upgraded missile, hoping for the upper hand. "When exactly are you willing to get on board on this one, Frank? The train is leaving the station, and you are going to be left on the platform. I hope I'm being clear." This, of course, often leads to nothing more than mutual frustration and very little positive movement.

Another common tactic is to sidestep the attack by gaining support in a more covert fashion. "Interesting point, *Frank*. I wonder if someone has a *different* point of view in the room?" While appearing attentive, you try to move the spotlight off the dissent by enlisting support for your own point of view. Your goal is to move away from the conflict and quietly shut down the dissident individual.

This strategy also rarely works, because what the challenger typically wants is to be acknowledged. The thinking goes like this: If we differ from our colleagues and do not feel heard, we'll usually continue to speak our mind. Most of us don't want to feel alone, so when we're isolated from our group, we'll want to repeat our message louder and more vociferously until we recruit some support. It's the American model—"If at first you don't succeed, try, try again."

The consequence of exclusionary behavior is that those pushed away only become heightened in their own feelings. Their sense of personal dignity will be hurt, and though they may say nothing at the time, their anger and pain will typically go into an "emotional vault," where it will sit accumulating interest until it can be withdrawn—often explosively.

A third option is this: Try moving *against* your instincts when an inflammatory statement is made. I learned this from my colleague, Sandra Janoff, the coauthor of *Future Search* and a leading expert on collaborative change. She taught me that in a group when an individual voice of dissent is expressed, it is important to fight the natural tendency to ignore or refute it.

Take a deep breath and offer an inclusive response that joins with—agrees with—some part of the statement. Agreement in part does not mean that one agrees in whole. However, it does mean that we do not leave a voice hanging out there alone, no matter what.

For example, try responding with, "Interesting perspective, Frank. Is there anything in what was said that someone can agree with?" Hear a few supportive comments and only then shift to alternative points of view. Time and again, I've seen contentious individuals start to shift their perspectives simply because they have been acknowledged. Sometimes, that is all they want.

In any form of communication typically sits the same need—the desire to be heard and appreciated. Responding at that level, and *only* that level, can quickly shift resistant and ingrained perspectives.

Tenkan teaches us that conflict is a little like standing waist-deep in the ocean at the very place where the surf crashes. Our initial tendency is to grimace and brace ourselves against the force of the waves. But if we choose instead to dive into the breaking surf and move against our natural instinct of either confrontation or dismissal, we can move forward easily, with minimal struggle.

TRY THIS . . .

- The next time someone raises a tough, controversial issue you disagree with in a meeting, see if you can "join" with a part of their position.

- See where the conversation goes.

DB

TAKE SOMEONE'S BALANCE

The law of Probability Dispersal decrees that whatever it is that hits the fan will not be evenly distributed.

—Unknown

In aikido, when someone is dead set on an attack, an interesting response is to "take her balance." On the mat, this means we literally go to where her body is not, and shift her balance by taking advantage of her rigidity. For instance, if attacked hard from the right, step in close to her left and with a small movement create an imbalance in her focus and force her to change approach. By not engaging directly in the attack and sidestepping it, we *turn* the assault from rigid to fluid.

In a human interaction, we can use the same approach of taking someone's balance by carefully noting the tone and intention of the communication.

Have you ever been in the following situation? In a meeting, someone raises her hand and out pops the following question: "Why don't we seem to care more about line staff?" The question leaves you in a defensive position, a bit flabbergasted and unsettled.

"Why, of course we care" you start. But the look on your face shows a little shock and discomfort that's translated into lack of surety. The asker is subtly smirking, drawing a line in the sand, and silently demanding an instant response. The old saying "Never let 'em see you sweat" isn't working. You have lost.

Why?

You were "attacked" in a manner that prevented any real possibility of response or resolution. The goal was not to discuss or resolve the issue. Instead, the goal was to try and surprise you and create a position of power and one-upmanship. Sometimes this is conscious; oftentimes it's not. The results are always the same. The strategy worked, because the query did not allow for any positive movement or resolution. There was no room to reach common ground. You become essentially "pinned" by a demand, held fast by an indirect statement imbedded in a question.

Interestingly, the opposite scenario is also possible. Sometimes, we can become pinned just by an irresolvable statement alone. For instance, your boss out of the blue and staring in your general direction says, "Our customer service was *very* disappointing this month!"

What can you say? "No, it wasn't!" Not likely. Shift into therapist mode with "You sound upset"? Only if you are not particularly interested in keeping your job. Again, you have been handed an impossible point with a delivery manner that did not allow for movement or resolution.

In both cases, however, you have the option of taking someone's balance. This strategy works effectively, *because* the positions held are rigid and inflexible and not in spite of it. Taking someone's balance means we step out of the way of the attack and effortlessly respond with the *opposite* posture. On the mat, we do not engage in our opponent's rigidity but seek a position that is 180 degrees from her delivery method.

This means, if asked an irresolvable question, reverse the query by asking for the statement. If you are the target of an aggressive statement, flip instead to a question.

In the first case, if challenged by a question, reversing it with a request for a statement helps to get at the hidden position in the query. Feeling "stuck" is often a result of knowing there is a strong, *unacknowledged* point of view. But because it's unacknowledged, it's impossible to respond to and thus create movement. When unspoken, this strong opinion basically leaves one shadowboxing, trying to dance and weave from an unknown assault.

The response is simple. Calmly say, "It sounds like you have a point of view. I can respond more effectively if I hear your statement. What is it?" In the previous example about supporting line workers, you might hear: "Well, I believe we don't value our staff. In fact, *I* don't feel particularly valued." This is now an opening you can react to for further dialogue and possible resolution. The door has been opened for a more honest and forthright interaction.

In the opposite situation, when attacked by a statement, try reversing it with a question. Consider the boss's challenge about customer service. The simple oppositional response is to say, "Robin, I can understand you are upset about service. I really want to take action, but I don't know what to do with your comment. Can you ask me a question I can respond to instead?" What you have done is to shift your boss away from a rigid positional stance into a potential dialogue. She might respond by saying, "What I'd like to know is what can we do to improve order fulfillment times?" Now you have something to work with, and a discussion has just been initiated rather than a one-sided, closed encounter.

A fine point to using both techniques is to notice how you made a subtle request for what you wanted. In the first scenario, it was: "It sounds like you have a point of view. I can respond more effectively if I hear your statement. *What is it?*" In the second, you directly said: "*Can you ask me a question I can respond to instead?*" Both times you made sure you asked for what you wanted.

The time to use "taking someone's balance" is when you are feeling stuck in a tough situation. Your instincts will tell you when to apply these techniques. Just remember, the next time you are feeling challenged but not sure why, it's likely you are facing an irresolvable attack. It's irresolvable because its nature does not allow for forward movement or resolution. This feeling of being pinned is a consequence of having literally no wiggle room. When this happens, try taking someone's balance by using the energy being given and doing the opposite.

TRY THIS . . .

- When you feel yourself pinned in a conversation, see if you can step away from the interaction.

- If pinned by a question, seek the statement in the moment.

- If held by a statement, go for the question.

DB

ATTACK THE EBBS

As long as we have some definite idea about or hope in the future,
we cannot be really serious with the moment that exists right now.

—Suzuki Roshi

In our business, we consult with organizations to make them more effective in their working dynamics. Our belief is that success breeds success. A good process will usually continue to build momentum for continued good development. It's the fundamental nature of our work. If we can help teams or organizations to have productive, valuable meeting experiences, logic dictates that one positive meeting will help to foster further growth. The simple question "What happened that made this so effective?" will generate lots of positive learning. It's common sense. So common, in fact, that it's the same model used by therapists and parents. At a basic level, we know that humans learn through success, and so we do everything we can to foster success.

However, it's important to realize that the converse is not always true. A difficult session, filled with antagonism and bad behavior, doesn't always lead to a downward spiral of fear or recrimination. Often, a really negative meeting can set up a positive change in the near future. And the worse the event, the more effective it can be for creating a significant transition.

This is an important component of *tenkan*—the knowledge there is a dance of time and energy that creates opportunities for deep change. It's the realization that a seeming loss can, with time and natural human dynamics, turn into a huge positive. But this can only happen if you are looking for the opening and attack the opportunity.

Case in point: I was running a board retreat for a prestigious private school in California, one of the oldest and best in the country. In attendance was not just the board, but also the school heads were there to help implement actions carried forward. Although I was aware of some tensions regarding certain recent school decisions, no amount of homework could have prepared me for the uproar that occurred.

Somewhere towards the end of the day, when everyone was tired and off-guard, the meeting went to hell in a handbasket. Barely contained animosity and frustration, held in check all day through politeness, erupted into thinly veiled accusation. Everyone's rabbit ears went up, as certain board members spoke of their anger over key decisions they were not consulted on. The headmaster tried to smooth things over by apologizing, but the damage was done. The school heads, already feeling disenfranchised from the board, stared at the floor and muttered among themselves.

Caught completely off-guard, I barely managed the dynamics in the room. I did my best, but the recovery was tough. The meeting ended with the board chair calling for calm and the desire for teamwork, but an evaluation at the end affirmed what I already knew: the meeting was a disaster.

As luck would have it, a regular board meeting was scheduled for two nights later. The chairman was deeply concerned about the negativity of the retreat and wanted to cancel the meeting so "cooler heads could prevail." I convinced him that sometimes the best time to make movement is when the tensions of the recent past leave members raw and exposed. It is in that exposure that a sense of embarrassment can allow for new openings in change.

It is an observable pattern with our clients that during a tough meeting filled with bad behavior, the next one is usually followed by an increase in civility. It's a sort of ebb and flow of human dynamics. We don't want the world to think of us as jerks (even though we may act the part) and so are somewhat contrite following outbursts of poor performance. A kind of remorse sets in. Capitalize on these moments. See them not as frustrating times but as potential opportunities to take your team to a deeper level. The secret is to trust in the incoming tide of good behavior and move forward just when the tendency is to retreat.

The board chair, not convinced, left me with the following admonition: If Monday's meeting continued the tensions of the retreat, my relationship with them was over.

In a nutshell, there was a difference of perception. The chairman's was that the risk was huge and that action was dangerous. I, on the other hand, believed that the past behavior created significantly *lower* risk—not in spite of it, but because of it. The time to attack was now. While the immediate tendency would have been to follow the board's lead and postpone the meeting, I needed to trust my instincts based on past experience.

OK, I thought. Time to cowboy up.

I started Monday's meeting positively by quoting Angeles Arrien.

"The two most magical words in the English language," I said, "are *next time*. We have a chance to be different. The choice is yours."

I modeled a positive approach by clearly conveying a calm and optimistic posture and holding to a closely facilitated style. I was not going to let the group degenerate back into its recent form. I was also sensitive to avoiding any hint of criticism that might make members feel judged. They could do their own internal work on that one.

Although on the outside I was smooth water, inside I was praying mightily that I had made the right decision. In truth, without the chair's full support I was deeply concerned. As it turned out, I had pushed for the right thing. As a consequence of feeling badly about their behavior from two days earlier, major movement occurred. The meeting was the most successful board meeting anyone could remember, both in tone and positive action. One tough board member, in a remarkable moment of contrition toward the school heads said, "We really want to work with you, and I'm sorry for my behavior on Saturday." You could have heard a pin drop. After that, it was smooth sailing. People were bending over backwards to make progress, and as a result former tensions melted into the air.

The lesson is clear: Be aware of the human tide of self-recrimination. There is a natural tendency to want to be better following a difficult event. *Tenkan* teaches us that the dance of the battle is one with ebbs and flows. Treat each event separately and stay open-minded that your attackers may change their stance based purely on their own need to change overly reactive or ineffective behavior. Fight your natural instinct to retreat following such a contentious event, and instead attack quickly with positive framings and optimism. Sometimes, the greatest change occurs when the situation seems most hopeless. Create an opening for such a turnaround rather than get locked into a negative reaction pattern.

Can you prevent lousy meetings from occurring or contentious employees from disrupting your organization? Of course not. Human beings are both at their best *and* worst during change. But realize that every disaster can potentially be an opportunity because of the nature of human contrition. Will you turn it around every time? No! That is just plain wishful thinking with no basis in reality. There will be some fires that continue to burn no matter what you do. But more, many more, will end well if you attack tension with a positive mind-set and advance when all instincts say retreat.

TRY THIS . . .

- For one month, end *every* meeting you run by asking two questions.

- "What did we do in this meeting that worked?"

- "What could we do differently next time?"

DB

KILL THE ENEMY

Out beyond the world of ideas of right doing and wrongdoing there is a field. I will meet you there.

—Rumi

In his book, *After the Ecstasy, the Laundry,* Jack Korn-field tells the following story:

"Once on the train from Washington to Philadelphia, I found myself seated next to an African-American man who'd worked . . . for a rehabilitation program for juvenile offenders in the District of Columbia. Most of the youths he worked with were gang members who had committed homicide.

"One fourteen-year-old boy in his program had shot and killed an innocent teenager to prove himself to his gang. At the trial, the victim's mother sat impassively silent until the end, when the youth was convicted of the killing. After the verdict was announced, she stood up slowly and stared directly at him and stated, 'I'm going to kill you.' Then the youth was taken away to serve several years in the juvenile facility.

"After the first half of the year the mother of the slain child went to visit his killer. He had been living on the streets before the killing, and she was the only visitor he'd had. For a time they talked, and when she left she gave him some money for cigarettes. Then she started step-by-step to visit him more regularly, bringing food and small gifts. Near the end of his three-year sentence she asked him what he would be doing when he got out. He was confused and very uncertain, so she offered to help set him up in a job at a friend's company. Then she inquired about where he would live, and since he had no family to return to, she offered him temporary use of the spare room in her home.

"For eight months he lived there, ate her food, and worked at the job. Then one evening she called him into the living room to talk. She sat down opposite him and waited. Then she started, 'Do you remember in the courtroom when I said I was going to kill you?' 'I sure do,' he replied. 'I'll never forget that moment.'

" 'Well, I did,' she went on. 'I did not want the boy who could kill my son for no reason to remain on earth. I wanted him to die. That's why I started to visit you and bring you things. That's why I got you a job and let you live in my house. That's how I set about changing you. And that old boy, he's gone, and that killer is gone. So now I want to ask you, since my son is gone, and the killer is gone, if you'll stay here. I've got room, and I'd like to adopt you if you let me.' And she became the mother of her son's killer, the mother he never had."

This is a powerful and remarkable example of the Mohawk strategy called "kill the enemy." We learned this concept from Terry Dobson in his aikido book, *It's a Lot Like Dancing.*

The Mohawk believe that an effective way to resolve conflict is to employ a similar approach as modeled by this extraordinary mother. To the Mohawk, when a disagreement occurred that could easily escalate into fierce conflict, they moved with deliberate speed and action to "kill the enemy." They would gather anyone who knew the individual or group and then proceed to name all the characteristics they liked and admired in them. They never focused on the dislikes— only the likes. They would also speak on the similarities they had with the "enemy" and the specific ways they were liked by others. As the process evolved, the Mohawk would find it more and more difficult to have ill will towards someone whom they had grown to admire and respect. Even if they ran out of ideas, they'd keep the conversation going, sometimes for hours, until the feelings and energy towards the "enemy" changed.

Killing the enemy to the Mohawk meant killing off the feelings that stood in the way of a peaceful solution. As a strategy, it's a powerful technique for resolving outer conflicts by focusing on the internal ones created by the tension.

In their unique way, the Mohawk were *tenkan* masters.

Tenkan teaches us that in conflict resolution the biggest battle is our internal struggle. How we see the other, the reputation he or she may have, or the tendency to polarize into right versus wrong are all problematic for a successful resolution. Like ballroom dancing, if you change your step or rhythm, it will literally force your partner to change theirs. It is the nature of any relationship. Conflict, whether we like it or not, involves another. And so, by definition, conflict involves a partnership—a good partnership or bad partnership is up to you. It is a relationship that begs for collaboration.

In a troubling relationship at work, spend some time doing what the Mohawk did and "kill the enemy." Consider all that he does well, positive traits, and the help he can provide in reaching your goals. Solicit input from others on where this individual or department has contributed in the past, and like the Mohawk, be vigilant to focusing only on the positive.

The more important the relationship, the greater amount of time you should spend on this strategy. And if you think this is fairy-tale thinking, a kind of nonsensical "feel good" approach you can never use with a serious issue, I ask you to consider the mother of that slain child. Living in a tough neighborhood, probably surrounded by poverty, her son slain for no logical reason—yet she rose above her pain and judgment to change her dance and create a remarkable result.

If she can "kill" her enemy, given all she's had to deal with, so can you.

TRY THIS . . .

- Consider someone you have a lot of trouble with and spend at least 20 minutes creating a list of everything you admire and respect in him.

- Find a trusted colleague and share your list. Does your perspective change?

- Take action from this new place of understanding.

DB

COUNT ON SILENCE

I try to keep my mouth shut and let people think I'm an idiot rather than open it and remove all doubt.

—Mark Twain

I have a client at Metropolitan Life Insurance with a most unusual negotiating style. During tough meetings, his position is to stay silent as long as possible. His strategy is one arguably perfected by the Japanese. He knows that silence is a powerful motivator to create movement. The longer he stays silent during meetings, the more he finds the other side of the table will increase the flexibility of their position.

This is because in our culture we are generally uncomfortable with silence. We equate it with boredom or anxiety, and it increases our internal tension level. Our typical Western response is to assume nature abhors a vacuum and thus to fill it with words. This, of course, is the last thing that needs to happen. Instead, the use of silence can be extremely effective at creating movement in situations ordinarily missed.

Here's an example: You're leading a typical meeting. "Winkle presented an interesting view of the new marketing department. I know it's a little controversial, and I really need to know where you all stand. So I'd like to ask what thoughts or questions you have regarding this new proposal. Do you have any concerns or objections?"

The group has that deer-in-the-headlights look. You can't get them to talk if their lives depended on it. The more tension that exists on the issue, the less likely anyone will be to jump into the fray. It's perceived as too vulnerable a position. Your team's strategy is to run silent, run deep, and live to fight another day.

After waiting the obligatory nanosecond, you say, "OK then. I'll take that as support. Let's move on."

And that is that.

Whether out of your own anxiety or the mistaken belief that everything is truly fine, you've just made a big mistake. A critical issue that needs to be fully aired has just been tabled due to speed and/or anxiety. Your people, sensing a missed opportunity, leave the meeting with their hidden concerns and resistances. The covert battle is on.

There is, however, a simple alternative. Use silence to creatively move a group through its initial fears.

I have learned over the years to use silence and the tension it creates to elicit input and engagement. For example, typically at some point in any meeting I am leading, I will ask for input or reaction. I am sure this is true for 95 percent of all meetings you may run. Every time I ask a question requiring a response, however, I do the following: I *slowly and silently* count to 15 as soon as the question leaves my mouth. The more challenging the question, the longer I wait. I let silence build the tension in the room, maintaining a placid expression but one that says, "I've got all the time in the world." As a consequence, I usually get engagement on tough issues.

Sometimes, I may have to wait quite a while. And sometimes, I need to wait a second or third time after an initial response. But since I am committed to waiting until the group responds, I typically get involvement. Once the ice breaks, the flow of input is always astounding. I am amazed at the "hidden" information that springs forth once a team starts really talking.

Tenkan teaches us to use silence as a way to invisibly move a situation forward. The tension that others feel in silence is a useful advantage, if you can learn to control your own tendencies. The challenge as a leader is to manage your own internal anxiety and not to jump in too soon. If you are uncomfortable with silence, your tendency will be to "carry" the tension in the room and react too quickly. That's why counting to 15 really helps. It has something to do with your mind and hands (remember, keep them in your pockets) that allows silence to work for you.

As is typical of any new skill, practice helps. Fortunately, practicing silence can be done anytime and anywhere. But the truth is that for many fast-paced leaders in wild, chaotic environments, silence is a rare commodity. That's why we recommend leaders spend 15 minutes in silence every day, so that it becomes a friend rather than a challenge. You can do this very simply. Find somewhere you can be by yourself and just sit. That's all. Just sit. Be quiet. Watch what comes up and observe. Don't act. Don't do anything but breathe and watch how you deal with silence. If you become impatient, just continue to stay in silence. Your task is simply to be comfortable. And if you are like most people, that will take time and practice.

What inevitably happens is that as you use silence to create movement in your team, the team will begin to respond more quickly to your expectations. This expectation builds momentum, so that down the road when you ask for a response on a tough issue you are more likely to get it. Your team will learn that a run silent, run deep strategy will rarely work when you are more than willing to be patient.

A final word of caution: The purpose of why you use silence is critical in the end. Intentions of "winning" ("I can wait out anybody in this room for as long as it takes") will be seen and felt ultimately as a power play and thus manipulative. This will not help your cause. There is a fine line between the use of silence as a competitive posture versus one where your team feels they can voluntarily engage in a deeper conversation and consciously avoid glossing over a topic that needs to be addressed. In the end, even though there is a tension that comes with silence, it must be felt more as an invitation and less as a challenge. Thus, check your intentions carefully, because your people will inevitably know.

TRY THIS . . .

- The next time a hot issue comes up, respond by not responding.

- Instead, let silence be your response, and let it guide the next steps.

DB

SHARE THE PAIN

It is in sacrifice that we lose ourselves, our pain, our problems.
It is in the sacrifice of self, for something bigger,
that life gains meaning.

—Sara Harrison

Doug Ayers, CEO of Coldwell Banker Residential Brokerage of Chicago/Milwaukee, one of the largest real estate companies in the country, told me the following story: "I had a girlfriend once who moved into my home. I came home on the day she was to move in and found she had taken all my furniture onto the driveway where it was mixed with all of her furniture. At first I was shocked. Then she calmly told me the plan—we were to mutually decide what would go where. Rather than fit her furniture into my place, we jointly decided what would and wouldn't work. Our 'new' home had a combination of her belongings and mine. And, we each had to give up something. At the time, I was a little put off, think-

ing, Whose name is on the mortgage? In hindsight, I came to
understand what an incredibly valuable lesson it was for me,
one that I use to this day as I grow and develop my company.
It is this: Share the pain."

This lesson, learned at an early point in his career, carries
Doug today in his exceptional leadership with Coldwell
Banker. As an organization, it is in a high growth and acquisition mode. Coldwell Banker went from $3 billion in sales in
1999 to $12 billion in 2001. The company is buying real es-
tate businesses left and right, large and small. Doug has been
building a unified culture by following his credo—share the
pain.

He recognizes that in any acquisition (and many though
not hostile were less than welcomed) there are chickens and
foxes. The foxes know who they are. The chickens know
who they are. There is no kidding any one. All the rah-rah
premerger meetings don't hold a spoon of credibility when
it comes time to parceling out the three "Ps"—privilege,
power, and perks. And the chickens, knowing this, will
oftentimes do their best to mess with the foxes.

For example, in Doug's case he needed to merge over 70
offices, all with different cultures and some strong competitors with each other. To create this "new" and productive
environment when merging offices, he considered a few
options.

One option was to relocate everyone to a new environment and go to a third location. This was a legitimate choice,
because there would be no familiarity or comfort with the

new space, and it would force a fresh perspective from the whole team.

Another option was to simply change management. The benefit would be a total rebirth of an office. A new, unified culture could be developed with the same discomfort shared in dealing with changes in leadership. In essence, everyone would feel equally benefited as well as inconvenienced.

While Doug considered both possibilities, he was in a bit of a bind. His goal was a less wholesale type of change. His primary intention was to both preserve capital while leveraging existing business opportunities. To achieve these two objectives, he decided on a third option. Mindful of his girlfriend's lesson, Doug decided to move the merged offices into one of the *existing* locations. He believed this option required an even greater level of "sharing the pain." He handled it in the same way his girlfriend handled her move—by "reshuffling the deck."

His strategy was this: Instead of trying to fit the new group of agents into the existing agents' space, he moved *everyone* out of the current office. Then he reestablished the group in their new locations based solely on criteria everyone could see was fair—sales production. The highest producer of the blended group got the best space and so on down the list. It was that simple.

An added benefit to this strategy was a more blended office where individuals interacted as a new group versus in the cliques from their previous offices. Truly, everyone involved shared the same pain.

Doug explained later: "Our strategy was to focus communication on the criteria for how things were going to be done. We created new and blended procedures and policies that involved everyone. And, we continued to create situations where the new group interacted frequently until they felt like one. The key for success, of course, was a real and perceived belief that the pain was shared by everyone, regardless of which office they came from. The only thing that mattered was their record. After that, we reshuffled the deck in an equal fashion."

Tenkan teaches us that when trying to make significant movement and minimize resistance, it is essential to understand where the sacrifices will be and to share the discomfort that will be felt. Make sure everyone knows two things. First, how you will be making your decisions, and second, when those decisions affect people in significant ways, it is done in a fair and equitable manner. In times of change, sharing the good and bad is critical to a sense of overall fairness that minimizes resistance and maximizes transition.

TRY THIS . . .

- During a difficult change, ask your people to jointly come up with recommendations on how to "share the pain."

DB

A SHORT NATURAL HISTORY
OF FEAR AND RESISTANCE

No one will manage his or her time in such a way as to free it
up for something they didn't want to do in the first place.

—Marty Cohen

As a consultant on accelerated change, I have spent my professional career coaching executives to deal with the almost-daily issue of organizational resistance. In some ways, the ability to effectively move an organization forward through pushback is what separates managers from leaders. It is this simple: Managers manage process. Leaders, on the other hand, get people to do something they probably might not otherwise undertake. That is why they are leaders. If employees did what was asked of them in the first place, that's not leading. That's moving a procedure forward and managing expectations. But leading requires by definition dealing with the inherent struggles that emerge during any change intervention.

Once you know the root cause, the potential actions you can take become easier to identify (but never easy). While resistance is usually a challenge to deal with, at least it's simple to understand. All forms, from passive-aggressive procrastination to outright belligerence, can usually be traced to one thing—*fear.*

Fear can take many forms, but the most frequent are fear of failure or its corollary, fear of being hurt. Consider the example of trying to teach your kid to do something new.

Your child will rarely explore new territory, if she potentially will be embarrassed, hurt, or punished. If your child feels she will fail, resistance goes up and the ability to get her to "try it" becomes a parental power struggle.

Well, guess what? Adults are no different. The more pain we anticipate, the more resistant we become. No rocket science here. We're hardwired that way.

Imagine an aikido practice session where you are trying to learn a new technique with a partner who is using too much force. She is so focused on technique that she tends to lose awareness of you, her partner. As a consequence, your wrist ends up bent in ways it was never intended, and you experience pain. Because of this experience, you then become overly watchful and rigid. Your resistance rises with the fear associated with self-protection.

As a leader, your strategy is to find ways of minimizing the fear your employees may be feeling. Don't just rush into action. *Tenkan* teaches us to first circle the issue before moving for a solution. Take some time to explore the underlying concerns your people have. And don't be surprised if some of these fears appear irrational and/or out of left field. Remember this: Emotions don't know logic. Your job is simply to address the underlying fear and not to judge it.

A simple model to hold in your head is to try to manage for "excellence" rather than "perfection." The difference between the two is this: Excellence incorporates mistakes, while perfection doesn't tolerate mistakes. If your employees feel you operate from a perfection model, then fear of punishment, failure, pain, and humiliation will run rampant and with it an increase in resistance. If, however, they feel you model excellence, their willingness to engage more fully in the change will increase.

All learning requires course correction. If your people are not making mistakes during change, you know one of two things. Either they are not making any mistakes (which means they are not growing, changing, adapting), or they are just getting really good at covering them up. Both should be unacceptable. Instead, consider the words of Barclays Bank Chairman Matt Barratt: "Mistakes are the natural price we pay for progress."

Of course, we are not advocating minimizing accountability and consequence if goals are not met. We want real rewards and penalties. But it's a fine line to walk. *Tenkan* teaches us that without real consequence for nonaction, there is sometimes not enough energy to break through the resistances that emerge. This means an occasional "slap upside the head" is needed to break a resistance pattern. This is what consequences do best. But if the consequences are all an employee feels or they are too severe, he or she won't accept responsibility. And we lose the battle to this emerging fear.

Finally, remember that people don't resist at the same time and in the same way. There is a cycle, a rhythm that can appear with resistance, and it is wise not to get caught in its illusion or appearance. Try to suspend your judgment by managing your first impressions of your staff. Experience has shown us that bad guys can become good guys over time and vice versa. Remember the tortoise and the hare? As in aikido, business teaches us it's not how we start but how we finish.

TRY THIS . . .

- During an organizational change, encourage excellence by asking your team periodically the following two questions.

- "What mistakes have you made recently?"

- "What have you learned from them?"

- This direct questioning encourages a culture based on learning rather than on self-protection.

DB

FORGET ABOUT CHANGE, WORRY ABOUT TRANSITION

Nostalgia isn't what it used to be.

—Unknown

A famous University of Southern California study examined the way the human mind thinks. It found the following remarkable result: The average human mind spends approximately 40 percent of its time thinking about the future, essentially worrying about those things that have not yet happened. Approximately 35 percent of the time is spent thinking about the past, in essence worrying about those things that have already happened and that we cannot change. That leaves only 25 percent of our time to focus on the present. The way we think can significantly impact how we see a changing environment.

Oftentimes, people talk about change as if it's the major internal issue. It's not. The way we see it, change is the external factors affecting our life. Change is what happens to us. It is situational.

What most people are talking about is "transition," the internal, psychological process we use to get right with the change. Thus, the definition of change is the external factors impacting us—the world events that come to bear when we wake in the morning. On the other hand, transition is what we do with that impact.

It's an important distinction, because many people talk about needing to "deal with change," when what they really mean is they need to better "transition" with the changes they are given. Control over the externals of life is a fantasy. We can no more choose life's changes than we can choose to walk on the moon. Influence? Sure. But control? It is the highest form of hubris to believe that one.

So how do we move forward with what we are given in a way that is positive to our spirits, our relationships, and our organizations? In a real sense, it's a state of mind. *Tenkan* teaches us to create opportunities for movement through timing and partnership. When that mindset of *tenkan* gets "stuck," it becomes almost impossible to create forward movement.

We know of a very bright academician who couldn't make the emotional shift to life's changes. In a previous job, he had been a Harvard instructor. When giving a student's paper a grade, he always gave two. The first was what the student got, and the second was what the student *would have gotten* at Harvard. Needless to say, he wasn't a very good teacher. He had never made an effective transition to his new life. Was it the change to another university that caused the bad behavior? No. It was the internal transition that caused the response. This is the way it almost always is.

Tenkan teaches us to forget about what is happening off the mat and worry instead about that which we have control over—our actions on the mat. It's the back-and-forth dance that takes a longer view of any problem. Too much time and energy in leadership are spent worrying about managing issues that we cannot control.

The next time you find yourself or your team embroiled in a difficult issue, consider responding to *only* that which you can control. Stay away from continually reconstructing the past or future fantasizing. Evaluate your previous decision paths; however, be mindful to manage the tendency to spend large amounts of time away from the present. Ask yourself or your team, "Right now, this moment, what can we address? What do we have influence over and can impact?" If you find yourself time traveling either in your mind or in your discussions, you know more than likely you are engaging in the change rather than focusing on the transition. Focusing on the change will always take you into past emotion or future worry. Focusing on the transition will instead bring you to the present and help provide focused, honest assessment.

TRY THIS . . .

- Consider creating the role of a "here and now monitor" for your meetings.

- His job is to keep the team from engaging in too much backward or forward talk.

- When the team goes offtrack his job is to ask, "Yes, but what can we do right now?"

DB

SEPARATE THE PAST FROM THE FUTURE

The past is a foreign country: they do things differently there.

—L.P. Hartley

A while ago, I ran a two-day strategic planning retreat for a well-known university. It was an organization I was new to, and though there was a fair amount of preparation to get me up to speed, my sense was it would be barely enough. As it turned out, it wasn't even close.

Almost immediately, the meeting conversation became filled with subtext and code. Participants were using catchall phrases to signal past hurts and issues that were known only to insiders. As a facilitator, I felt like I was watching a foreign movie without the subtitles. Coded messages dressed up as heat-seeking missiles were aimed from one group to another over past organizational tensions. Although the meeting had a very clear purpose, design, and stringent ground rules, with the energy present I felt like I was riding a Brahman bull. Day one ended just the way I expected, with frustration and tension. Worse, for someone who usually feels very confident in sessions of these types (and with an excellent track record of success), I was feeling bewildered. I felt like I was swimming in molasses. The confusion was such that I literally couldn't track what was going on. And I'm usually pretty good at tracking. It's what I get paid for.

The day ended with less than enthusiasm for day two. Unless I could get a handle on the unnamed but ever-present thorny issues that floated around the room, we were all in big trouble.

It wasn't until the next morning, after a good night's sleep, that I fully understood what happened. I had made a major tactical mistake. The mistake was this: We had mixed the past with the future, a very common but potentially deadly error.

When doing strategic planning, it's important to separate the *organizational issues,* which are usually all about the problems of the past, from the *strategy,* which is about creating a compelling future. There is a natural tendency in any strategic planning process to want to talk about the issues, which will only take your organization into a time machine of hurt and anger. In planning, it's critical to hold the line so that past issues don't interfere in future conceptualizing.

Please note: We are not advocating that past issues never be addressed. Organizational tensions need to be fully vetted and explored to find out how and when they may block future progress. But, they should not be brought forward into the early stages of effective planning. That is potential suicide.

Why? Well-known researcher Ronald Lippitt found that when people focus on past issues they get depressed. This is because they often move into patterns of blame or insufficiency. This self-inflicted tension tends to create an energy whirlpool of frustration and tension. The past then haunts the present by draining energy, time, and goodwill.

But Lippitt also found that when individuals or groups focused on the future, the opposite happened. They got energized, excited, and positively focused. They became captivated by possibility, rather than failure, and reacted accordingly.

Tenkan teaches us that leading strategic change is about allowing the right issues to emerge at the right time. This means fighting the natural tendency of almost every group we have seen to engage in "problem identification" as an early part of planning. As a leader, your job, and it's a tough one, is to hold the line on this instinctual response. Instead, allow the dance of past and future to occur in proper sequence and deal with reality only after the preferred future has been created. Do this by creating clear guidelines that do not allow for past concerns to surface unless you request them. Otherwise, past issues will tend to drag you down in your process, and it will be hard to overcome the typical anger and resentment that occurs from rehashing old issues. In my experience, this will initially require "hard" facilitation on your part. But once the group sees the value in not going over old territory, it usually becomes freer and energized by the shift in thinking, and will start to manage its own backwards-looking behaviors.

This is what happened in the meeting on day two: I explained my theory of what happened and set ground rules that wouldn't allow for discussion of the past (even if the past was yesterday). I was clear to set a specific focus on future talk and close the door on any discussion of past hurts or problems. When participants occasionally regressed and raised past-related issues, I quickly came in and reminded everyone of the ground rules. Though the group was initially resistant, as we created movement in the group's work, my strategy gained greater credibility.

As a consequence, participants momentarily were given permission to free themselves from past attachments and with great excitement jumped into future visioning. The meeting's outcome far exceeded anyone's expectations. As a group, we built a compelling future for the university that later served as a positive context for dealing with the tough problems that originally plagued it. Only this time, there was both a positive history of success as a group and a magnetic future in which to balance out its anxiety. Today, the group is well on the way to both its vision and solving its tough issues.

TRY THIS . . .

- During your next planning session, segment the meeting into three distinct parts.

- Part one *only* assesses the past.

- Part two *only* discusses the future.

- Part three *only* focuses on action.

- Make sure the three sections stay separate, and the conversation doesn't get pulled back into the past.

DB

DEATH AND RENEWAL

You are what you have learned from the past, what you experience from today, and what you dream for tomorrow. When you become reluctant to change, remind yourself of the beauty of autumn.

—Unknown

One of the joys of living in New England is the beauty of the seasonal changes. Of particular note is the autumn, when the leaves of deciduous trees turn bright colors of red, yellow, and orange. Fall is a time of year of almost constant commentary in our small town. Almost every day starting in mid-September, the question "When do you think it will be peak?" is heard among neighbors. It's the time year after year when Mother Nature puts on a spectacular show. And you'd be hard pressed to find one person in our town who doesn't look forward to this magnificent spectacle. Looking at a mountain of bright reds and yellows, it's easy to feel inspired and hopeful for the world.

But the scientific truth tells a different story, because beautiful fall leaves actually mean they are dying. The process of fall stops chlorophyll from being created, and the leaves lose their green, eventually to whither and drop. Even though the implication is of a kind of death, we accept this. We don't try and glue the leaves back on the trees. We trust that a "death" of one type brings renewal of another.

William Bridges, a leading international voice on transition, has made a lifetime of study on this subject. One night at dinner he told me: "The problem with the human experience is we have memory lapses. We see in nature almost every day that death and decay in one form always bring renewal of another. Always! It happens all the time. The loss of one job allows another to appear. A painful divorce allows a new, more loving relationship to be possible. A health crisis and its loss of mobility can create opportunities for healing relationships with family members. Even the death of a loved one can open doors in one's life—turning pain into a fruitful and valuable experience. But this memory lapse makes us less trusting of this natural pattern. What is true in nature is equally true in our own lives."

Listening to Bill's words that night I thought back on my own life. Like many, it was filled with divorce, health crisis, and career transition. It became blindingly obvious. Bill was right. What was also painfully clear was that at a basic level, I didn't trust the seasonal experience of my own nature, that year after year the cycles of change, given time and distance, always brought renewal. But fundamentally, every time something went wrong, with every chaotic event, I thought, This will never turn out well. This is nothing but bad news.

I decided to really test Bill's assumption a few weeks later. During a workshop I was leading for 150 people, I asked everyone to think of his or her worst personal or professional experience. Once identified, I then asked, given time and distance, did it eventually become a positive experience? Finally I asked, knowing what they now know would they trade their current existence for their old pretrauma life?

The answers astounded me. I heard stories of cancer, job loss, catastrophic accidents, and even rape and the death of a young child. And almost all, with little exception, found the experience to be positive and illuminating in their own life's journey. There were, of course, a few voices that wanted their old life back, but a huge percentage, many more than I would have ever thought, were happy with the way things eventually turned out. Even more stunning was that the majority of those wanting their past life back said they believed, given time, they too would embrace the changes.

Tenkan teaches us that in every situation exists two distinct pictures. The "now" of what currently exists and the potential of what we will learn if we take the long view. During your next challenging time, remember that renewal is a natural by-product of ending or a death of some kind. Welcome the opportunity that already exists in nature and probably in your own personal history.

TRY THIS . . .

- Consider some of your most challenging times, both personally and professionally.

- Then ask, "Did everything turn out for the best?"

- If the answer is "yes," take this awareness and try to apply it to a current frustration or challenge.

- What could be a positive outcome if only you took a longer view?

DB

IRIMI

THE SINGLE SWORD STRIKE

WHAT IS IRIMI?

Move like a beam of light, fly like lightning,
strike like thunder, whirl in circles around a stable center.

—O'Sensei

Irimi, or the single sword strike, delivered by the hands of a master is an impressive sight to observe. There is no separation of sword and person; they move as one. The concentration and focused energy are palatable. In order to be successful, each swordsperson must connect and pay close attention to every movement, breath, and shift of grip of the opponent's sword. A break in concentration or a held breath indicates an opening for an attack. The sword strike happens in an instant, a flash of energy. Some people say a perfect sword strike sings. Even to an untrained ear, you can hear the "whoosh" as the blade slices through the air. The result is undeniable. It only takes one or two sword movements to neutralize an attack. *Irimi* is economy of motion with maximum results.

The four-direction sword strike practice is at the root of hundreds of aikido movements. Senior aikidoists at some point in their career may do the "thousand cuts" practice, where they perform 1,000 sword cuts in a row. After several hundred, you realize that you can't raise the sword with only muscle and that you have to relax enough to access *ki,* a universal energy source. Any imperfection of your technique is painfully obvious. The sword practice, though, is more about deepening your ability to be calm and focused, expanding your skill in bringing all your power to bear on an opponent, and your ability in decisively resolving a contentious situation.

In the business world, *irimi* has an important place on the path of effortless leadership. How a leader exercises power can either create struggle or unleash the potential of an organization. What is the connection between understanding a problem and taking action? Can a leader balance compassion and decisiveness? When necessary, can a leader shift the attitudes and actions of an entire organization with only a few powerful, well-timed comments or actions? There are *irimi* techniques that give a leader this potential.

THE THREE IRIMI TECHNIQUES

1. Pursue relentlessly what is at the heart of important business issues. Create an environment where all employees continually investigate the root causes of success. What is at the heart of our customer's satisfaction with our products or services? What is at the root of our product quality problems? Provide for some emotional distance by reinforcing the guidelines of no finger pointing or blaming. Slicing through to the heart of your business prevents the organization from only addressing superficial symptoms. Pay attention to both the emotional and energetic reaction of your colleagues. When people are just intellectually debating symptoms, the energy in the room is diffuse. When you have discovered the truth of the issue, you can hear a pin drop.

2. Take bold action. Bold decisions are enacted with 100 percent commitment and with no hesitation. Full resources are devoted to the plan, and everyone involved knows that it is one of the top priorities. Too often in the corporate world, decisions are made that are then retracted, underfunded, or approached with an "if we get there, we get there" haphazard attitude. In *irimi,* either you move with boldness or you don't move at all. To start a sword strike halfheartedly or with hesitation results in instant failure.

3. Be concise. Irimi emphasizes economy of motion. What is the one sentence that captures the imagination of your organization and slices through a tough business issue? Less is more. Too many words dilute the power of your message. You need to provide enough context, with the understanding that people get lost in a lot of words. Bring all of your emotion and energy to that one sentence for maximum expression of power. Another variation of this technique is to use silence, following a compelling message, to create movement in your organization.

Timing and connection are other important techniques. Listen for and sense the moment when your people are most open to being influenced. Is the pain of the situation or the potential enticing enough for them to be willing to change? Share your ideas at an energy level that your direct reports can easily receive, which can be different from what you may want to express. You don't want to blow them out of the water or soft-peddle your message to the extent they don't get it. The greater the impact of your decision, the more connection you need with your colleagues. Indiscriminate sword strikes cause damage. Are you using the right level of power and timing in your bold decisiveness to allow your direct report to hear, be moved, and stay centered?

Irimi in the workplace provides focus in today's fast-moving, complex environment. There is an economy of movement that places resources where they can best make a difference. Harmful interactions are respectfully diffused and eliminated before they become dangerous power struggles. Seeking the truth and boldly taking action with right timing and power lead to effortless leadership.

JH

KEEP THE STRIKE SIMPLE

Everything should be made as simple as possible, but no simpler.

—Unknown

A number of years ago I took a trip to the Grand Canyon. I try and make it a point, whenever I am within 100 miles of its range, to go for a social call. It's great therapy. I find that if I am feeling the least bit overimportant or impressed with the magnitude of my personal problems, a good 20 minutes staring into the canyon's abyss will certainly fix whatever ails me. And if for any reason I'm having second thoughts about the majesty of nature, well, those 20 minutes will certainly fix that as well.

The Grand Canyon makes me weak in the knees. It makes me gasp. It starts a tingling in my toes that by the time it reaches my shoulders has turned into a full frontal shake. It is just that strong a presence for me.

The weather in early May at the Grand Canyon can be unpredictable and surprising. The day I visited was unusually warm and misty. With snow still on the ground mixing with the warm drizzle, an unusual situation was created—the Grand Canyon was fogged in! I mean, I literally couldn't see 15 feet in front of me. Though directly below me the canyon dropped away thousands of feet, there was nothing to see but mist. Standing on the precipice was like peering into the middle of a cloud. I walked back and forth around the rim, staring into the dense fog, trying to see something. The problem was there was nothing to see. It was fog, fog, and more fog. After a while of back-and-forth rim pacing, reality began to slowly set in. Let's face it. One goes to the Grand Canyon for the view. When there's no view, there's not a lot to do. So I ended up doing what everyone does when the Grand Canyon gets fogged in—I headed straight for the gift shop.

As I poked around the gift shop, a guy walked in who immediately made his presence known. He was beside himself with anger and frustration. I had never actually seen this before, but his veins were literally poking out the side of his neck. It was impressive, if not a bit unnerving. Talking to no one in particular, but directing his attention somewhat to a small Navajo woman behind the counter, he started right in.

"I can't believe this. I've waited over 40 goddamn years to see the Grand Canyon. This has been my dream for my entire f**kin' life. My dream! I finally have the time, take a bus trip here from Florida . . . and it's fogged in. I've been here for six hours, the bus is leaving in 15 minutes, and I haven't seen a thing! Not one goddamn thing!"

The spittle forming on the sides of his frothy mouth punctuated his rage. Like most people in the store, I was trying to find a safe distance from his fury. His eyes squinty and fixed were rabid and a bit scary. He looked like he wanted to bite the head off a small mammal.

But the little Navajo woman behind the counter held his gaze kindly, without the smallest hint of fear. She stood silently for a moment, seeming to gather herself. Then she did the most amazing thing.

Leaning forward she gently took his hand. Then quietly, but firmly, she spoke directly to him, holding his gaze in her eyes. She said, "I can understand that sometimes the Grand Canyon gets fogged in. But what I can't understand is that you would devote *only* six hours of your life to your life's dream."

Immediately the man deflated. His eyes opened wide, his shoulders sank, and the emotion he was carrying dissipated into the thick fog waiting outside with the bus. I have no idea what he was thinking, but whatever it was clearly went right to the marrow of his bones. He left the store dazed and in complete and total silence.

In all my years, I have never seen a better example of the single sword strike. The anger of the man was immediately transformed into a lesson he will never forget. Its long-term value is unknown, but this *irimi* master beautifully modeled the "moment," the ability to instantly reframe another's beliefs.

Irimi teaches us to bring forward focused energy, timing, and intention for the single sword strike. But a key element of *irimi* is to keep the strike simple, to go to the heart of the issue. When engaged in a fierce sword battle, there isn't a lot of time spent on the way someone is dressed, the conditions of the area, his size relative to you, and the quality of his sword. All is superfluous to the action occurring. What is essential is the half-second strike that changes the battle. That is all. Comment and/or debate will not alter that. In fact, it will be a distraction from what needs to be done and is potentially harmful.

Our Navajo *irimi* master knew the battle wasn't about the fog or the weather patterns or the waiting bus. It was about the abandonment of a personal dream, and the price that is paid for doing so. This is what she focused on exclusively—that and nothing else, not the man's rude behavior, insulting language, or intimidating manner. Our master attended to the one issue that had the highest priority. It was the entire content of her strike.

When considering *irimi* be careful to manage any temptation to either pile on or focus away from the essential. Instead, ask yourself, "What is the heart of what needs to be said, and how can I say it in as few sentences as possible?" A single sword strike is just that. It is not an ongoing flurry of activity. It is simple, clean, and quick. If it's the right action or words, any addition will only complicate and diffuse the impact.

The next time you are considering *irimi,* call up the image of this small Navajo master behind the counter at the

Grand Canyon gift shop. Then modeling your actions accordingly, keep the strike simple.

TRY THIS . . .

- The next time you need to deliver critical feedback, see if you can go right to the heart of the matter with both firmness *and* kindness.

- Keep the message to two or three lines.

DB

BOLDLY SEIZE THE TEACHABLE MOMENT

The reason lightning doesn't strike in the same place twice is because the same place isn't there twice.

—Willie Tyler

In every changing organization, there are teachable moments that can have a huge impact. They are often symbolic, significant, and with enormous potential. Frequently to an outsider, they don't seem like a big deal. But internally, where insiders know the game, these actions can have huge implications to the culture and spirit of the business.

Here's an example: Barclays Private Banking is one of the oldest and most venerable institutions of its kind in the world. They are counselors and money managers for those individuals of great privilege and wealth. Their clients are, by definition, very, very rich. When you enter the bank's building in London, you are struck by the "tone" of the place. It oozes with confidence and old English protocol. The place *feels* moneyed.

But like many businesses in London, it is short on space, and there is a constant battle for any open opportunities. In a give-and-take world of compromise, Barclays is no different from a thousand other organizations—all needing more room with no feasible way of getting it.

It is with this as a backdrop that the following remarkable leadership moment occurred.

My client at Barclays was the managing director, William Oullin. New to the organization, William was a seasoned and talented manager. He had an impressive track record of success with another bank, where he was known for the combination of people and technical expertise he brought to the table. But William was running into significant resistance in his desire to change the business. First was the old Barclays Private Banking culture—a very traditional and somewhat elitist model. When combined with the previous authoritative top-driven way of running things, William inherited a cumbersome and resistant business line.

During a critical three-day all-leadership meeting with his top 65 bankers, a teachable moment occurred. It was the window of change he had been looking for to make an impacting statement, and it had to do with the issue of client conference space. There just wasn't enough of it. The private bankers simply didn't have a high-class lounge to meet with their wealthy clients. They had conference rooms, but nothing that reflected the Barclays cache.

Of course, the nicest space in any bank building typically belongs to the top executives. Barclays was no different. In this case, Chairman Lord Robert Fellows, former secretary to the Queen, resided in the center of the building. And William, the managing director, was in a beautiful corner office. It was the way it had always been and probably would always be—space or no space problem.

While others complained about the problem, William saw the opportunity for a significant teachable moment. At the end of our meeting, he committed to one simple action. Starting the following week, he would give up his corner office to Lord Fellows. Lord Fellows's beautiful office would be used as a client meeting lounge. And William? He would find a new office that was more visible and in the heart of the business. His goal was simple: to make an important public statement that said, "I am serious about changing our culture. I will do it by giving up a symbol of privilege for us to use with the customer. Watch me!"

However, William wanted to be careful in his solution. He did not want to simply take an employee's workspace for his own, which was contrary to the culture of mutual support he was trying to imbue. Taking a subordinate's office would only create a different space management issue as well as possibly diminish her status. Instead, he wanted to send a powerful message—that status and rank were not dependent on where you sat, but on what you did and how you acted. He wanted to be seen as an up-front and visible leader, not one who was traditionally closeted away in a far-flung corner office.

His response was brilliant.

William Oullin, managing director of one of the oldest and most respected private banks in the world, had his office built in the hallway in the most visible and least prestigious spot he could find—between the bathroom and the elevator!

At Barclays, where form oftentimes preceded function, the impact was immediate and profound. The "buzz" around the office was extreme disbelief. There were bets placed on how long he would last in this new space. No one could believe it. But William, recognizing the value of the teachable moment and the importance of symbolism, told me he would "never leave this space," because it modeled everything he was trying to change. And if he couldn't lead by example, how could he ever expect his people to follow on the more significant issues of compromise and teamwork.

He laughingly told me one night over dinner, "There should be no question in their minds where I stand regarding the value of the customer over the importance of role and status. They will know it when they arrive in the morning, when they leave at night, and many, many times during the day."

In *irimi,* the goal of a single sword strike is to lay waste any resistance by demonstrating complete and full-hearted commitment through action. William's symbolic gesture, timed impeccably and with the exact right issue for the organization, challenged the traditional culture while solving an old, historic problem. The price paid was the loss of a large, comfortable office. But what was gained was a quantum leap in credibility for him and an almost breathless response from a formerly resistant organization.

Irimi teaches us that good leadership looks for these symbolic moments every chance it gets. On average, you may get 10 to 15 such chances a year, if you are lucky. An effective leader is aware of the existence of these moments. But an extraordinary leader, like William, actively seeks to create them and boldly models change with quick and decisive actions.

TRY THIS . . .

- Consider an important cultural value you are trying to bring forth into your organization.

- Then create a visible, permanent change that will signal your support and belief of this value.

DB

CREATE THE COMPELLING DECISION

A great leader must know and understand himself. A great leader must know and understand the times in which he lives.

—Benjamin Disraeli

Executives currently talk about the need for "compelling market strategies" or a "compelling vision" that would define their business. They issue a call to action, a way to rally the troops towards a common goal. Their hope is that if the vision is compelling enough, employees will take on the cause and focus their efforts towards company success.

Interestingly, Webster's has two definitions for *compel.* One is "to drive with force," and the other is "to drive together." That is an important distinction that can make or break successful implementation. Is the leader "driving with force" to accomplish goals, or is he "driving together" with employees to create success?

In aikido, the use of force creates resistance and unnecessary struggle. Merging intent and energy to drive a solution together allows for greater results in a more effortless process.

Here's an example: Tom is the new vice president of network infrastructure at a large corporation. His monumental task is to integrate and consolidate the network and computer systems worldwide and across a variety of separate companies. He has to partner with the business heads in order to create both the plans and implementation at the local level. Often, the divisions have had their own IS people and have built their own unique systems over the years. This situation offers the best and worst dynamics of any matrix line-staff relationship.

During the first several months in his new job, Tom took the time to carefully assess the opportunities. He got a lot of input from both the line and staff groups. There was a huge opportunity to both improve service and dramatically reduce costs. It didn't take much of a Power Point presentation for senior management to endorse his plan. That was the easy part.

When Tom and his managers started unveiling the plan to the divisions, they hit a brick wall. There was resistance

from line managers who wanted to keep total control of all
their projects and systems, fearing that, if consolidated, Corporate would take over. Some offices felt their system needs
were too unique to integrate into a global system. Others
claimed that they didn't have the time to focus on another
project. It was clear that the plan was not compelling enough.

Tom's first response was to go back and get more facts.
The business case for the scope of the systems consolidation
wasn't strong enough, and the line managers were viewing it
as arbitrary and another Corporate strong-arm tactic. They
were experts at subtly resisting—many corporate projects
had died a long, slow death due to stonewalling and neglect.

Rather than issue a corporate edict that would garner resistance, Tom calmly said that he felt there were valid reasons
to pursue the project. But until there was an undeniable business rationale, he would present the project as "optional"
(with certainly a strong endorsement) for the business units
to adopt. Two months later, Tom returned with such a con-
vincing case that senior management declared participation
by the divisions was nonnegotiable.

Most managers would have delighted in picking up that
"big stick" to bully their line counterparts into compliance.
But Tom took a different approach. Quietly, calmly, and with
an air of mutual respect, he restated the business case, citing
how much money it would save the organization without
compromising service. Adding a new twist, he stated his
commitment to go back to senior management to get their
approval to upgrade technology. It was something sorely
lacking and much needed by the divisions.

One by one, the divisional groups came around. They were impressed by his willingness to listen and to advocate for technology upgrades. His line colleagues couldn't resort to their usual resistance tactics, because Tom wasn't reacting to them. Each time they pushed back, Tom would restate the purpose, the upside for the organization, the fact that it was nonnegotiable, but ultimately it was their choice. The case was now becoming compelling.

Two other actions unseated the last remnants of resistance. First, Tom quickly focused his team on line managers who agreed to participate in the consolidation project. These clients got fast response and uncompromised service, better than they had received from most corporate groups. Secondly, he quietly announced that in three months the additional costs generated because a division had not participated in the consolidation project would be allocated to that division. This created a lot of attention. Tom employed this tactic last. He knew if he started with cost allocation it would come across as a threat. Once the business rationale was compelling, it made sense that a division should be held accountable. The outcome? Within six months, all the divisions were on board, the company eventually saved millions of dollars, and the level of technology was upgraded.

Irimi teaches us that using the single sword strike in the workplace requires a compelling rationale for taking that action. A business case is compelling when the facts are undeniable, the action rises above the politics of the organization, and people "feel" a call to action. As a result, resistance seems to dissolve. Too much energy is wasted trying to force decisions that aren't compelling. As a leader, you have a choice to drive a compelling project together with your colleagues or resort to using force to implement a decision. One leads to effortless results, the other to potential struggle and resistance.

TRY THIS . . .

- Think about the top three priorities for your organization.

- List the business rationale that justifies the importance of each goal.

- Then ask yourself, "Is it compelling enough?" Be brutally honest.

JH

SPEAK YOUR TRUTH WITHOUT BLAME OR JUDGMENT

The sword has two blades: the blade that kills and the blade that heals. Which will you use today?

—Samurai saying

A friend and client, Paul, was hired as CEO to help a small, privately owned technology company expand its business globally. It had a great product, cutting-edge design, but had never expanded beyond a few industry applications. Paul brought the much-needed business development expertise and a network of helpful contacts. It seemed like a perfect match of skills to launch the company to the next level.

At the helm of the company and its board was the chief technologist, the brains of the company, and its leader from the beginning. Initially, Tony loved the idea of hiring Paul, so that he could ease into semiretirement, spending more time in the lab and less focusing on day-to-day operations. Unfortunately, things didn't turn out according to initial expectations. Although he expressed his desire to reduce his involvement in the business, Tony never really relinquished control. He would sit in the back of Paul's executive team meetings and openly critique his ideas. He would also circumvent Paul to make decisions with the manufacturing group about product release dates. When Paul confronted him, Tony would attempt to undermine his confidence. He suggested the rest of the executive team was uncomfortable with Paul's leadership, and that he needed to wait longer before making any bold decisions about changing the operations.

Paul sought counsel from board members who, in private, agreed with his perceptions about Tony sabotaging his ability to lead the organization. Their typical responses: "It will just take Tony a while to let go" and "Be patient. Tony just takes things personally. When sales increase, then he will back off." They agreed with Paul, but were not willing to take on Tony at a board meeting.

During the first year, things improved, but not much. Tony was unpredictable, supporting Paul on a certain initiative and then outwardly resisting him on what would normally be a tactical decision. While on vacation for a month, Tony's absence gave the organization a chance to fully adjust to Paul's leadership style. Progress was being made: new products designed, global business partners identified, marketing campaigns launched, and financing arranged.

Then out of the blue, Paul got a call from the board. Tony was asking that Paul be fired and wanted to negotiate a severance package. Paul, although not totally surprised by Tony's actions, was stunned at the sudden reversal of support of the other board members. Tony was trying to mandate this decision, and an emergency board meeting was set up for that weekend.

Feeling set up for failure from the beginning by Tony, Paul's initial reaction was anger. His family had just settled in after relocating, and the thought of uprooting them again was frustrating. He had spent a lot of time building relationships in the company and was really excited about the company's future. Just as the plan was beginning to yield results, the rug was pulled out from under him.

He also knew that he could never be successful in the CEO role unless the board fully backed his decisions. Without the board's active support to address the dysfunctional behavior of Tony, Paul would never be able to lead in the bold and decisive style that the organization needed. It was time to detach from his dream of leading the company to the next level of success. This was clearly not the best place for him, and he began to let go of the CEO role. To stay in the job would compromise his integrity.

Paul could have quietly resigned and taken the severance package without much fuss. He could have alluded to Tony's power play to his colleagues, giving them just enough information to discredit Tony and the board. Paul had developed credibility with the workforce as someone who knew the industry and really cared about the company. His words carried weight.

It was important that Paul address the situation with full integrity. The first action he took was to engage a lawyer, so that, if needed, he could initiate a wrongful dismissal lawsuit. Paul knew that the board of directors didn't need exhaustive data to fire a CEO, but he wanted the board to have to grapple with the facts rather than simply acquiesce to Tony's demand.

Second, he prepared for the emergency board meeting by pulling together a compelling business presentation about the state of the company. There were several key business deals that were about to be closed, in which he was intimately involved. To change CEOs at this moment would potentially put those deals at risk. Paul wanted the board to take full responsibility for the timing of its decision.

Finally, Paul took bold action at the board meeting by openly addressing the impact of Tony's actions. Careful to be at *full-powered presence,* Paul used *irimi* to respectfully talk about the unpredictable interference and undermining effect of Tony's interactions. He was quick to point out the occasions when Tony was supportive, but laid out a case that transcended their relationship. Paul stated that, while he was greatly disappointed and it was difficult not to take these events personally, Tony's actions represented a pattern that would sabotage any CEO. Paul was calm, candid, and simply presented his case. The board listened quietly, including Tony who uncharacteristically did not openly challenge him. The board thanked Paul for his comments and adjourned to a private session to discuss its decision.

Afterwards, Paul felt at peace. He hadn't colluded with Tony's tactics, he had spoken his truth, and he had made the right decision to maintain his integrity. By detaching from the situation and emotionally accepting the possibility that he may have to leave his job, he was able to be more courageous.

Speaking the truth from a place of power and integrity becomes a perfect expression of *irimi,* the single sword strike. According to Angeles Arrien, it is essential to separate truth from blame or judgment. In order to do that, you need to take full responsibility for your part of a situation, apologize if necessary, and detach from those interactions or relationships where you cannot be effective or your integrity is at risk. The most invincible samurai warriors were those who were absolutely willing to die. From this stance, rebuttals, revenge, and resistance seem like petty and futile reactions to this type of honesty.

Our example of Paul is a wonderful model of how to do *irimi* right. He courageously addressed the CEO–Board leadership issue without colluding with a power struggle or by attacking and blaming Tony. With *irimi,* he spoke his truth and, in the process, gave the board ample information to make a much-needed change in the company. Unfortunately, they were not as courageous as Paul. He left to start up another venture, and they hired a CEO who will most likely find himself in the same power struggle with Tony down the road.

TRY THIS . . .

- Identify a situation where you must take a stand.

- Accept the possibility that your wisest choice is to disengage from the project or interaction.

- Then without being attached to the outcome, state your truth without blame or judgment.

JH

GET UNSTUCK
THROUGH PENALTY

My motto? No pain, no pain.

—Carol Leiffer, comedienne

What's often needed for either getting unstuck or helping others in the process is a firm and measured kick in the ass. In my experience, the benefits to not changing are so deeply rooted in one's fear patterns that something totally anathema to the individual is often needed to break the unconscious benefits that keep one stuck. The benefits to not changing are oftentimes so strong that they provide an insurmountable force to action. Without these benefits, movement would be a graceful affair.

Somewhere, somehow a gain prevails that keeps the individual tied into a long-standing and painful cycle. Without addressing these benefits in a creative and forceful manner, their power is often hypnotic and stubborn.

What then can be done? How do you respond quickly to such a difficult situation? In aikido, the direct response would be called *irimi*. *Irimi* is a set of techniques that requires boldly stepping into the heart of an issue to slice through any patterns that either prevent clear expression or threaten harmony. *Irimi* is about breaking that which is not life affirming. In the most dramatic of cases, an *irimi* move will cut *ki,* or the life force, of the other individual, because the continuation of her pattern is life threatening for them or others. It is always done with respect and compassion.

It is the spirit of *irimi* that gives us a strategy for action. Sometimes, the only way to enable real movement is not through providing benefits or "positive motivation" but through the mitigation of patterns through pain.

If many well-intentioned efforts have failed, we can be successful in working with change by focusing on the "negative" side of transition. Sometimes, *irimi* is the only way to break the unconscious barriers. We can do this by creating scenarios that are *worse* than the fear of breakthrough. We make *not changing* so highly undesirable that it outweighs the risk *to* change. Individuals need to feel that the current state of nonaction is more painful than movement. The question becomes how?

We've found a very effective strategy, somewhat controversial and unique, but very potent. It is the spirit of *irimi*. We use a "penalty."

Case in point: I have a friend who for three years had been struggling to get the first chapter of his dissertation completed. No matter what he did, he was constantly finding excuses and reasons for delaying the task at hand. This put him in a desperate situation, because the more he delayed, the worse he felt about himself and the more he would procrastinate—a typical vicious cycle.

One day I said to him, "Bob. Do you *really* want to get this done?"

"Yes," he emphatically implored.

"Terrific. How much is it worth to you to get your first chapter completed? Five hundred dollars? A thousand dollars? Five thousand dollars? Be real but aggressive."

"Oh God, I'd pay $5,000 to get it going."

"Fine," I said. "Write me a check for $5,000 and post-date it one month from today. If I don't have a first draft in my hand by this date, I will cash the check and send the money to the Republican National Committee (he was an ardent Democrat)."

My goal was to create something so painful he would rather have walked over burning coals than miss his deadline. He hemmed and hawed for a few minutes, but I kept repeating the question, "Are you really serious about this?" The more he protested his intentions for change, the more the idea seemed to be an obvious bellwether test. It was time to get off the pot.

The response? His fear of financial loss was overpowering. Five thousand dollars was a fortune to him at the time, representing a quarter of his life's savings. Add to this the fact that the money would go to the Republicans, and it was enough to break his fear patterns. Once broken through the use of a "penalty," his emotional energy propelled him forward. Bob became a man possessed. Finally free from the indulgence of his self-inflicted judgment, his creative energies went to a more productive use. He had the first chapter completed in two weeks and a finished dissertation in four months!

Could he have canceled the check and not met his obligations? Of course. But then he would have had to deeply confront his lack of commitment to breakthrough. And we agreed that if he took this action, he would never again be allowed to complain to anyone about his lack of completion (an almost nonstop topic of conversation). He finally would have to deal with the benefits he was receiving from not changing—receiving sympathy from all the pity he got for his "struggles." That in itself would have been helpful.

If it is a financial theme, it should be realistic but hurt. For some people, "hurt" is $500. For others, it's $100,000. This is a judgment call. In our experience, if there is a sharp inhale of breath when discussing the number, it's just about right. Penalties don't always have to be about money. I have used the technique of a penalty a number of times with other, more creative approaches. With one overweight client, for instance, who had historically *wanted* to exercise but could never "find the time" in his busy day, the penalty was to clean his ex-wife's house once a week for a year. He would rather have died than miss his goal of weight loss and daily aerobics. Today, 40 pounds lighter and with a healthier body, he attributes this creative penalty as the essential help needed for breakthrough.

Irimi teaches us to be judicious when using the penalty approach. If done for the wrong reason it can be punishing, only reenforcing a self-view of failure. It's very important to make sure the intention of a penalty is to support the individual and break that which cannot be broken in more supportive ways. A trusting relationship is essential. Without it, you will be perceived as cruel or manipulative. But at the right time and place with the right person, it can be a powerful technique for breaking through stubborn and long-standing intransigence.

TRY THIS . . .

- Consider something you have been trying to change for a long time but have been unable to do, such as lose weight, exercise daily, or change jobs.

- Create a realistic plan for yourself with a substantial penalty.

- Then get the one person you are least likely to be able to manipulate and let her in on it. Make her your support system.

DB

VERBAL ATEMI: THE "WAKE-UP CALL" RESPONSE

If you tell the truth, you have infinite power supporting you;
but if not, you have infinite power against you.

—Charles Gordon

Generally, aikido is a defensive martial art, aimed at protecting yourself and then your partner from further harm. One exception is in a life-threatening situation. The other is when your partner, caught up in the heat of the moment, becomes overly aggressive and can potentially cause harm to either of you. In this case, he or she needs a quick, well-placed strike to help shift attention back to center.

This wake-up call is called *atemi*.

For *atemi* to be successful, your timing must be perfect and your execution swift. *Atemi* is most effective before the attacker has fully completed his strike. Placement is also important, and finding that location where your attacker is most vulnerable is critical. For instance, if an attacker is overly aggressive with a right arm punch, he will leave the left side of the body vulnerable. This is an opening for an *atemi* strike.

The most important variable is the right level of power. Too little, and your attacker brushes it off like a mosquito. Too much, and your counterstrike escalates the conflict or causes harm. You want to use just enough effort to clearly get your opponent's attention, while surgically diffusing the attack. *Atemi* is the wake-up call of aikido techniques. It alerts your opponent that his aggressive intentions will not be successful and should instead be returned to a more balanced, respectful place.

Atemi in the business world is an important skill in effortless leadership. Think about those situations where you sense one of your direct reports is starting to build up a head of steam about a certain business problem. Your employee's opinion is starting to get more emotional. He or she is beginning to blame other colleagues or lose sight of the broader aspects of the problem. This is when verbal *atemi* is appropriate—before your report builds too much momentum and may cause harm.

To make you more successful with *atemi,* here are a few key characteristics to consider:

- If the timing is early, before the team or direct report has built up a head of steam, consider a *preemptive strike* that causes your employee to reconsider her approach *before* she crosses the point of no return or causes harm.

  For example: "Janet, before we step into the next meeting, I want to give you a heads-up about a controversial issue. Knowing your tendency to debate issues, I need you to help keep the meeting on track by viewing both sides equally."

- Your intention needs to be clear. The purpose of verbal *atemi* is to help your colleague rebalance and return to being her best, and to prevent further harm or struggle. Your goal is to help broaden your colleague's perspective if it's too myopic, become more collaborative if oppositional, or consider additional viewpoints if too rigid and one-sided.

For example: "Ellen, you and I both know how politically sensitive this project is. Please remember to address your concerns to the project leader instead of your colleagues outside of the project team."

- The *atemi* message is short, respectful, and to the point. Too many words come across as preaching. A condescending tone will embarrass your colleagues and create resistance. At its best, colleagues appreciate a well-timed, respectful, verbal *atemi*. This is because you hold their best interests at heart before they say something they will later regret.

  For example: "John, before you jump to conclusions about the project, slow down. Let's make sure we are considering all the facts causing the problem."

- Sometimes your intention can be conveyed with just a look or a gesture. One executive team I worked with knew that when the CEO carefully took off his glasses and placed them on the table, it was a signal that they had started to become parochial in their opinions and needed to return to a more collaborative tone.

- While respectful, your verbal *atemi* should also communicate that your message should not be ignored. You convey with words and energy that if there is no change in course, you will diligently take further action to advocate for the right response. *Atemi* stops short of becoming a threat that may cause employees to react from fear. Your *full-powered presence,* clear intention, and crisp delivery have a "snap out of it" quality and are not understated or diffuse in their message.

For example: "Excuse me! Before this discussion degenerates into a full-blown conflict, once again pitting product design against marketing, I want to remind everyone that our primary focus should be on what our customer needs for next year."

- Finally, use your report's name (or the client's name) right up front to grab attention and focus energy. The use of someone's name is a powerful method for gaining full attention.

Remember, verbal *atemi* rebalances an individual or team before going too far on a tangent. It resolves conflicts before they become too entrenched. Employees appreciate this *atemi* wake-up call before something is said they might later regret. Teams develop loyalty to leaders who can respectfully and swiftly address an unproductive, potentially harmful situation before it gets out of hand. Verbal *atemi* helps your direct reports be at their best.

TRY THIS . . .

- Who needs a wake-up call?

- Rather than procrastinating or colluding with a direct report's ineffective behavior, use a verbal *atemi* to help him or her self-correct.

THE TWO ESSENTIALS TO MOVEMENT

Either do not attempt at all, or go through with it.

—Ovid

In order for movement to occur in almost any situation, it requires two things—need and want.

Need is usually defined by the external factors that require a change or movement to occur. Need often looks like a changing demographic or a shifting environment. It is oftentimes defined by something other than desire that brings the change to the table. Consider the following statements: "I need to lose weight." "We need to improve our sales." "You need to hear this." Oftentimes, the need is something rarely summoned or desired. When the word *need* is in play, there is a sense of external demand and expectation, as in "We need to do something." This is not bad. It is often the first step to a reality of action. It is typically not pleasant and almost always unwanted. But it is necessary. However, the step of understanding or accepting need cannot be the end-all and be-all of movement. Because without the second building block—*want*—nothing usually happens.

Want is defined by desire. It is the internal drive for movement that fuels forward momentum. Want is all about our internal wishes. It is often psychological and propelled by benefit; that is, what benefits will I get by changing? Without it, without these benefits, nothing happens.

In our experience, leadership is usually very good at articulating *needs*. Company meetings are often filled with presentations on environmental challenges requiring action. Cases are often compelling and motivating. No expense is spared in getting the message out. But in presenting the needs, two critical mistakes are often made.

First, little consideration is given to the want in general. So much attention is given to the why *we* need to change (or the "need"), that the why *I* need to change (or the "want") is rarely touched on. Leadership often forgets to address the internal benefits that employees will receive through action. This is sometimes called the WIIFM, or "what's in it for me." It's an obvious mistake.

But more subtly, there is an inherent assumption made on the employers' part when they do address the *want*. Leadership sometimes assumes it knows what the *want* is—when in fact it oftentimes doesn't. Leadership may know it at a global level but not at a personal level. Rarely is the time taken. Based on this untested assumption, it then takes action or pitches its case with a mistaken and poorly told story. When the initiative results in poor performance, leadership shakes its head and wonders what went wrong.

One client, a large HMO, was changing information platforms. A huge investment had been made in new technology that would allow for the management of large amounts of complex data. In an age of increasing competition, information management was clearly the way of the future. Those companies that could get it and use it faster and cheaper were going to be the big winners. Those that couldn't weren't going to be around in five to ten years. It was that simple.

After making the decision to change IT systems, the CEO then mounted a huge internal sell campaign. In a se-

ries of half-day meetings, he blanketed the entire organization with a well-rehearsed PowerPoint presentation on the
need for change. It all made so much sense—the company's
competitive advantage, the positioning in the market, the
potential for acquisition—it was a thing of beauty. The only
problem was, it was exactly the same presentation he made
to the board. And the board's *wants* were very different
from the *wants* of those slugging it out day-to-day in the
claims department. He never once addressed their *wants.*
Not once.

When he started to hear about resistance, he was morti-
fied. How could this be? he thought. I've given them every
reason. He was dumbfounded.

When I was called in, the project was close to being la-
beled a failure, even before it went live. Within ten minutes
of seeing the PowerPoint presentation, I knew that the *wants*
had been poorly handled. We quickly regrouped. I asked him
to spend some time with his line employees getting their
view—no middleman, just him.

In 60 minutes of talking to his employees, he had a
whole new perspective. He followed his disastrous first session with a whole new round of presentations. This time he
spoke to job security, greater flexibility in hours, promotion
opportunities, and even the chance to get out at lunch for a
walk or better food than the lunchroom served. They loved
it, and a crisis was averted.

Irimi teaches us to ask two questions when trying to
create movement. The first question is, How do I answer
both the *need* for change and the *want* for any movement?
The second question is, How do I ensure that the *wants* I am

pitching are truly what my people want and not a projection of my hopes, concerns, or assumptions? Answering this question takes some effort on your part.

Clarifying both questions before taking action is an essential prerequisite to movement. If you can't, your battle may be over before the first strike.

TRY THIS . . .

- Before trying to implement a significant change, draw up a list of your key stakeholders.

- For each group, consider both its needs and wants.

- Determine how this can significantly influence your communication and implementation strategy.

DB

THE FINE LINE OF GIVING ADVICE

Compassion simply stated is leaving other people alone.
You can be available to another human being, provide
what they ask for, but it's a fallacy to think you
can impose your trip on another person.

—Ram Dass

There is a tendency, once you become familiar with the basic techniques in aikido, to want to share your new skills with any willing listener. After all, it has been a long, awkward road of practice with lots of trial and error, and it's nice to reach a plateau where things start to work. You're compelled to return the favor of helpful assistance, and although you won't admit it publicly, it also feels good to strut your stuff.

Blue Belts, those who are about half of the way to Black Belt, are most likely to become enthusiastic advisors and leap at any opportunity to "show you the way." And so they scan the mat for those potential recipients of their newly minted advice. Let's see, there are the Black Belts, easily identified by their *hakama,* a skirt worn over their practice uniform, originally intended to hide the feet so as not to tip off the attacker of their next move. They usually don't need technical advice. Beginners are also easy to spot because of their new uniform and that same wide-eyed look you had early on. Beginners are sponges for new information. Other than that, the only tip-off of a "friend in need" is when someone seems to be struggling with a technique. Advice surely would be helpful in order for them to get it right.

That's where the fine line of advice giving comes into play.

The fine line of advice giving highlights the *irimi* skill of knowing when to share suggestions, how much information is just right, and how to cater your assistance so it provides maximum benefit. In some respects, the same mistakes that overzealous aikidoists make are similar to the ones that leaders commit in the workplace. Our experience is that leaders, similar to Blue Belts, commit four common errors in their advisory role, and that *irimi* principles offer alternative approaches to those situations.

Situation #1: New employees want information to get started, understand the basics, and minimize confusion. But, too much advice at once gets in the way. Employees want advice in usable chunks, so that they can internalize one part at a time. If a leader gets too absorbed in the topic or just wants to do a data dump because he's too busy, his direct report will feel overwhelmed with details.

Provide advice to someone new at a task in small portions, logically and specifically explaining each procedure. Let him internalize each step before describing the next.

Situation #2: Beyond beginners, a common error Blue Belts make is to assume that if someone doesn't perform a technique well, they must want some advice. This good intention, based on wanting others to do well, is fraught with assumptions. The aikidoist may want to practice a move several times just to get the feel of it; his goal is not initial perfection, but instead to familiarize himself with the movement. Your words will serve as a distraction, not really usable until his curiosity is met. The person may be from another aikido school and is practicing a viable technique in a different style than is taught by your teacher. Not only does he *not* need your help, he will be offended by your arrogance that one style is better than another.

Ask first whether advice or another perspective would be helpful to another person before launching into giving help. Respect his decision if it is to decline your offer.

Situation #3: Another mistake enthusiastic advisors make is to assume how they learned a particular technique is the best way for another person to gain the skill. Some people are visual learners, others internalize new information by listening to verbal descriptions, and still others are kinesthetic, meaning they learn from physically experimenting with a new activity. Just watching a demonstration of a technique never was very effective for me. My preference is for someone to show me the technique and then stand by my side as I try the movement, giving specific feedback along the way.

If someone wants advice or help in learning, ask him what style of learning works best for him and then try to cater to that preference.

Situation #4: The fourth situation occurs when people confuse their love of problem solving and troubleshooting with helping another person. For example, a colleague may come to you with a business question like "Here's how I'm planning to deal with this customer problem. Am I missing anything?" You ask background questions, get intrigued with the situation, and before you know it, are enthralled with creating an innovative solution and proceed to contact "perfect people" in your network to assist. This may be helpful to the overall solution, but your colleague feels left in the dust and that you've taken over his project. Your zeal for troubleshooting compromised your advisor role. Most likely, that person won't ask you for help again, unless he wants to subtly off-load one of his responsibilities onto your plate.

Honor your colleague by providing just the assistance he needs, nothing more and nothing less. Don't let your enthusiasm for firefighting or troubleshooting overshadow his leadership role in the given situation.

Most Blue Belts go through an enthusiastic advisory phase and then realize that humility and respect go hand in hand with helping other people on the mat. They begin to understand that each person experiences aikido differently, and there is a wide range of motivations for coming to class. Well-timed and customized advice is a great gift. I can still remember key learning moments going back ten years. My friend Chris Thorsen helped me really understand "getting off the line," as we practiced after work in a park in Seattle. Finally, if offered from an attitude of humility and respect, advice is easier to receive and often more in tune with what the recipient needs.

Giving advice can be like the single sword strike of *irimi*. Nonnegotiable, critical information to new employees is essential to their jobs and should be communicated concisely and directly. Beyond that, focusing on exactly what advice your direct reports need, in what communication style, and in what depth is important to both develop their skill and confidence in managing that situation. Provide too much information, and they become dependent on your advice. Unnecessarily troubleshoot or give advice when it's not needed, and you will be viewed as a micromanaging and condescending leader. Your *irimi* advice should quickly and effectively meet their needs, so they can get great results.

TRY THIS . . .

- Review your intentions before giving advice and make sure you are really meeting the needs of your direct report or peer.

JH

THE POWER OF
TRUE APOLOGY

No matter how far you've gone down the wrong road, turn back.

—Turkish proverb

Before practicing a technique, aikido partners bow to each other. The bowing can be symbolic of many things, such as emptying the mind of knowledge so that new learning can take place or acknowledging the choice to practice with full commitment. It also conveys that both partners trust each other to practice in a way that creates no harm.

Occasionally, someone gets hurt, either by an overexuberant attacker or a partner who is too heavy handed in her response. After attending to the injury, both partners stop and bow to each other. The intent is to apologize to each other for creating harm. There is no blaming. Both partners take responsibility for the unfortunate circumstance and renew their commitment to being even more attentive and diligent in their practice. The environment of creating no harm allows for a higher trust level and freedom to elevate the practice level. If the full apology bow without blaming did not occur on the mat, then practice partners would harbor resentment towards each other, practice levels would become tentative, and the overall spirit would diminish.

Here's a great example: A key division of a major international bank was holding its annual international meeting in Paris. The head of the division was relatively new in his job. It had been an up-and-down year. The year had taken its toll. He had been trying to push his agenda of a unified business strategy in a silo-driven organization, and it felt like he was furiously bailing water from a leaky boat. His frustration with the territorial mentality of his organization had left him at his wit's end. From his narrow vantage at the top, he was convinced that most of his managers would deliberately try to sabotage his efforts, and that resistance to a new way of doing business was high.

As a last resort, he called his organization together to attempt one more try at gaining its support.

He opened the meeting by saying, "In my many years of experience, all I've ever wanted was to do my best. I am sure you want to do your best. I am equally sure our people want to do their best. And if we as leaders can't make it happen, then shame on us."

The trouble was, I was not sure he meant it. Although an important and valid message, he was feeling tense and sour regarding his manager's commitment to change. The message lacked punch. You could feel the underlying ambivalence. You could feel the discomfort in the room as well. No applause. No response. The meeting segued into hushed whispering, as the managers split into discussion groups to examine the tough issues standing in the way of the strategy.

As it turned out, it was a stunningly honest and thoughtful meeting. The normally reserved group expressed passion and feelings rarely shown. Tough issues were fully and honestly vetted. Yet the tone was surprisingly positive. It was a very creative and powerful session in which straight talk about hopes and dreams was shared. The head of the division had clearly underestimated his managers, and though exceedingly pleased with the results, felt embarrassed about his misperceptions and the condescending tone of his opening remarks. I asked him to address the group, to be honest and clear about the impact the meeting had on him as a leader. I was hoping for a thoughtful response. I was stunned by the impact of his words.

With all eyes on him in expectation, he simply said, "I have listened carefully to what you've told me today. I've felt like I've singlehandedly been pushing against a closed door trying to create change. But after hearing your views of the world, I've come to realize that I've been pushing against an open door all along. I'm sorry. I have been putting up barriers to your good efforts. It's time for me to take them down and change the way I have been seeing you. You are clearly ready to go. I just haven't seen it. And shame on me, if I can't get you there."

You could have heard the proverbial pin drop. The room was breathless. It was, as they say, the moment when everything changed.

What happened that made this remarkable session occur? It was a terrific lesson in *irimi*. At that moment, his group of managers had effectively diagnosed the barriers to success and was ready to champion the changes needed. The only thing holding them back was the head of the division and his misplaced frustration. Decisive action was needed to eliminate the leader's ambivalence, keenly felt by every manager. The single sword strike required in this case was full apology and full endorsement. By being honest, clear, and direct—placing no blame or judgment—and apologizing for his ac-

tions, the leader dissolved any last remnants of doubt and un-
leashed the power of his managers to implement the needed
changes. His use of full apology as *irimi* was more powerful
than any motivational speech.

TRY THIS . . .

- Go apologize—without explanation, justification, or
  defense. Trust us on this one. You'll have plenty of
  opportunities today.

- Put four parts into your apology: (1) what you did,
  (2) what you learned, (3) what you will do differently
  next time, and (4) what you need to do to reconcile
  the situation.

                                                      DB

THE STREET MUGGERS
IN YOUR MEETINGS

Big shots are only little shots who keep firing.

—Anonymous

There are a number of studies asking criminals to identify
the characteristics of an easy victim. Convicts are shown raw
videotape of a crowded lunch hour street, and they can pin-
point who they would attempt to rob and who they would
avoid. Their surprising victim list doesn't necessarily include
the elderly, women, or small people. Instead, muggers prefer

to go after someone who is preoccupied with his or her thoughts, walking tentatively, gazing at the ground, or engrossed in a cell phone conversation. In other words, the best criterion for getting attacked is to not pay attention to your surroundings and narrow your field of awareness.

In order to not get "mugged" on the aikido mat, you need to be at *full-powered presence* to maximize your awareness of incoming attacks and use *irimi* to quickly respond. Occasionally, attackers will have less than helpful intentions. For instance, they may give you a confusing attack, changing a strike midstream to really test you. Or perhaps, because of fatigue their attack is halfhearted. Maybe they get uncomfortable when their attack proves overly challenging and go easy so you look good, choosing to avoid conflict. In any of these cases, taking an *irimi* stance to quickly address these dynamics is important.

In the business world, a common place that leaders can get "mugged" is in meetings. Often running hard, a manager will step into a regularly scheduled meeting and attempt to drive an agenda. The typical scene is one of people arriving late, with mild confusion about the agenda, multiple conversations punctuating the discussion, and a rapid cruise through as many decisions as possible. Because the majority of meetings only serve the purpose of updating the team (and usually just the manager) or comparing ideas about an opportunity without actually making the decision, most employees learn that nothing of real consequence happens. The real decisions get made off-line.

On the other hand, when teams know their leader is genuinely interested in their involvement in a business critical decision, they take the meetings more seriously. And when the stakes are high, the meeting muggers can come out.

There are three types of meeting muggers who will attempt to derail your leadership: stonewallers, headwaggers, and saboteurs. Although their tactics are subtly different, their goal is to prevent bold action from being taken. Their common motivation is often based in the fear that they will lose something in the transition, won't be up to the new level of performance, or will leave the comfort of the old way of doing things. They are contrarians by nature and don't know when to stop debating and playing the devil's advocate. Sometimes, they just like to make trouble and watch a leader squirm.

Here are the three meeting mugger styles:

1. Stonewallers sit in icy silence, often in the back, and never volunteer an opinion. If asked, they will typically give cryptic responses. They won't overtly challenge ideas, but it's clear to everyone in the room they will stubbornly resist the plan. With great endurance, their goal is to starve bold decisions by preventing the energy the team needs to move to action. A stonewaller's motto is, "I can hold out longer than you."

2. Headwaggers are just the opposite. Like a plastic dog sitting in the back of a car, constantly wagging its head, these team members say "yes" to anything the leader suggests. On the surface, they are viewed as en-

thusiastic, verbally supportive, and positive team players who give no apparent resistance. But underneath, their strategy is to gloss over the important facts and discussion, so that the decision will be quickly made without any meaningful commitment to implementation. Leaders can become lulled to sleep, thinking their team is on board, when the consequence is a lack of action. The headwagger's motto is, "This too shall pass."

3. Saboteurs like to attack hard and fast. Using the excuse that only good decisions are made when different opinions are expressed, they relentlessly push their viewpoint. They will openly challenge the leader, interrupt their colleagues, and refuse to budge from their position. Saboteurs try to enlist other team members, sometimes putting them on the spot in the middle of the meeting, and try to gang up on the leader. Their goal is to use their assertiveness to achieve acquiescence, so that a bold decision is withdrawn. The saboteur's motto is, "I will wear you down."

The behavior of these meeting muggers represent the shadow side of helpful contributions your team can make. For instance, the effective use of silence to collect your thoughts is the flip side of the stonewaller's lack of participation. Enthusiastic verbal support is critical for a team to generate energy to implement a bold decision, not unfamiliar to the headwaggers. The flip side of the saboteur is to seek the underlying truth while respectfully and rigorously debating the tough business issue. Often, meeting muggers know they have a choice whether to be productive team members, and one of the variables to their personal decision is the approach of the leader.

Helpful team members may turn into meeting muggers, if they feel the leader is not listening to them, being arbitrary in his rationale for making a decision, or trying to force a rigid decision without sufficient input. These are common actions of resistance in response to heavy-handed attempts at control. These tactics also come out in a meeting when the team feels the leader is distracted or unsure. A leader who does not immediately use *irimi* to address the unhelpful dynamic also signals to potential meeting muggers that they have an easy target that day.

In addition to preparing the agenda and gathering pertinent facts for discussion, there are *randori* tactics that can serve leaders well in dealing with meeting muggers.

The first is to make sure before entering the meeting room that you are at *full-powered presence*. Center, take a few deep breaths, and expand your awareness to include all your team members at the table. Starting the meeting from this vantage point immediately sends the message you are not easy prey, are firmly at the helm, and won't be surprised by any covert action. You leave no opening to attack. Most of the time, as validated by the convicts watching the videotape, meeting muggers will choose another victim or another time when the leader is not centered. In the same way, meeting muggers will only resist when they think they have a chance of success.

Occasionally, a meeting mugger will persist. When this happens, use *irimi* to take calm but decisive action. For instance, the saboteur's contrary opinion needs to be acknowledged, not ignored. When a saboteur persists, ask if other team members have similar viewpoints. By this request, you create an opening for inclusion while modeling respect for differences. Trying to divert the team's attention away from the saboteur will only increase his resistance.

Headwaggers need to be slowed down in their superficial endorsement of a decision. You want to recognize enthusiasm for a decision but also encourage greater discernment about the implications. Focusing the discussion on the specifics helps ground the team and brings a dose of reality to headwaggers.

Finally, when dealing with a stonewaller, matching silence for a short period gives the message that you value team members taking time to collect their thoughts. If you are still met with limited response, then set the expectation you will solicit input outside of the meeting. This reinforces the expectations that all team members participate in critical decisions. Silence can be a very effective use of *irimi*.

Irimi and *full-powered presence* are potent defenses against meeting muggers. From there, (1) choose tactics that keep the group focused on the critical business decision, (2) genuinely solicit and acknowledge input from the team, and (3) strive to cocreate the solution. This will provide a clear leadership path for your team to follow, minimize resistance, and keep the meeting muggers at bay.

TRY THIS . . .

- Pick one of your regularly scheduled meetings.

- Consider the participants.

- Now try to identify any street muggers who may show up.

- Head off any possible inappropriate behavior by talking to them beforehand.

- You might want to think about the following question: "Am I a street mugger in any meetings I participate in?"

JH

HUMILITY KEEPS US CONNECTED WHEN USING POWER

If you stop to be kind, you must swerve often from your path.

—Mary Webb

Early in my aikido career, I had the honor of studying with Professor Takeshi Sairenji, one of O'Sensei's senior students and one of a handful of sixth-degree Black Belts and *shihans* (senior teachers) in the country. The opportunity to learn from a master who had personally studied with O'Sensei, founder of aikido, was never taken for granted at our dojo.

Off the mat, you would never recognize Professor Sairenji as someone so accomplished in martial arts. Soft-spoken and not a large man, he fit more of the microbiology Ph.D. image, the job for which he and his family had immigrated to the United States. On the mat, his stature seemed to double in size as he handled any attack with power and grace.

One evening at the end of class, Professor Sairenji asked the class to wait a minute before leaving the practice mat. He bowed to the class and then apologized for using aikido techniques off the mat. Both stunned and curious, the class did not know how to respond. Professor Sairenji relayed the following story.

The previous evening after class, Professor Sairenji had returned to his lab and found a teenager in his office. When he inquired whether this visitor needed assistance, he was confronted with, "Move out of the way old man! I'm taking your computer."

"Please, sir, I cannot allow you to do that. Several months of lab data are stored in that computer. Perhaps I can help you find another," Professor Sairenji replied.

"I'm not using your computer—I'm stealing it. Now move before I have to hurt you," the teenager threatened.

At this point in the story, there was almost a collective gasp in the class as we realized the impending doom of this teenager at the hands of one of the world's aikido masters. Wonder if he's out of intensive care? was the thought that crossed my mind.

"Sensei, what did you do next?" inquired Steve Kalil, sensei, his assistant.

Apparently, the teenager aggressively attempted to push Professor Sairenji out of the way. But in one swift move, Sensei avoided the attack and had the youth pinned to the floor. The teenager was clearly surprised, realizing he had severely underestimated his "victim."

"I suppose you are going to call the cops," the attacker said. This time, however, with a whole lot less bravado.

Instead, Professor Sairenji calmly asked his adversary why he needed to steal his computer. The teenager began to tell a story of being kicked out of his home by an alcoholic father, and that he was constantly broke. His part-time, minimum-wage custodial job at the hospital was the only job he could find. Forced to drop out of school, he had never been able to pursue his interest in science. He liked sneaking up to the lab to look at the experiments, and one thing lead to another. Now he was afraid that this conviction, based on previous brushes with the law, would lead to prison. They talked for over an hour, with Professor Sairenji kneeling next to the young man, comfortably but securely locking one of his arms, and the teenager lying face down on the floor, telling his life story to this older Japanese man.

In the end, Professor Sairenji let the boy go without calling the police. The teenager promised to change his ways and to reenroll in school. Sensei offered to help get him a job in the lab if he completed his studies.

At the end of the story, he once again bowed to the class. He held deeply the value of not using his martial skill indiscriminately off the mat. He genuinely wanted to know if there was anything else he could have done before resorting to pinning his attacker. Relatively new to our culture, he also wanted to make sure that his actions had not offended any of his students. We could only admire his intention and respectfully returned his bow.

Ten years later, this story still stands out as one of my most important aikido lessons.

First of all, Professor Sairenji demonstrated the critical link between humility and power. In this situation, he had every right and reason to trash the thief. He had been threatened, his attempt to mitigate the conflict was ignored, and he was potentially at risk. Most people would say he was entitled to use his power to save himself and his computer. The thief deserved it. Professor Sairenji's humility and deep respect for the power of aikido, both during and after the incident, were impressive. He deliberately chose not to use his power recklessly or to create harm. He took bold action, but only to the degree it was necessary to neutralize the attack, and not for revenge, self-satisfaction, or self-righteousness.

Equally impressive was his ability to stay connected to his adversary. He initially gave the teenager the benefit of the doubt and even maintained rapport after he was pinned to the ground. Sensei gave his opponent a chance to reconsider his actions, and he responded in a caring way when the young man began to open up about his personal troubles.

He never heard from the teenager again and ultimately didn't know whether he returned to school or to crime. But it is safe to say that if he had called the police and the boy had gone to jail, given the statistics of repeat offenders, the boy would have been back on the streets. By maintaining connection after the attack, he gave the boy two important messages. First, never underestimate another person, and second, if he wanted to realize his dream it would require a different path.

Too often in the corporate world, leaders forget that humility and power need to go hand in hand. With leadership and its associated power, the greater the need there is to exercise caution. A sense of entitlement or insensitive use of power creates harm in any organization and ultimately leads to resistance and struggle.

Irimi teaches us that to effortlessly lead, we need to be connected with our people before using our power. Even when taking decisive action with an opponent, hold her best self-interest at heart. Maintaining humility and connection becomes the symbolic bowing, communicating to our organization that we are willing to take bold action without creating harm. This "bowing" is what enlists the highest form of respect for any leader.

TRY THIS . . .

- Are you wielding the power of your position with humility?

- Does your leadership create the most good and the least harm?

JH

ANSWER YOUR CALLING

I believe we have two lives. The one we learn with,
and the one we live after that.
—Glenn Close, in *The Natural*

Gina knew when she was 26 that her calling was to be a dance choreographer. It was as if she had no choice. It gave her focus and purpose in life. Sometimes, it felt like an obsession, haunting her when she thought she needed to do something different.

Pam was a consultant for 20 years and thought she was ready for a change. She took some time off, traveled, and pursued interests that she never had time for when she was absorbed by her career. After a while, she realized that consulting was "in her bones," and she loved who she was when she was troubleshooting a business crisis.

Gary had been in the same career all of his adult life. He was good at it, and his job afforded his family an affluent lifestyle. There were moments of excitement, like when an unusual project with complex variables came up, but most of the time, he could do his job in his sleep. He felt trapped as his family's primary provider, but as he looked at himself in the mirror each morning, he wondered deep down if this career was really what he should be doing.

Steve was on his fifth career. Each time he had completely reinvented himself, from business manager to travel guide to writer to prep school guidance counselor. Now he was starting an online mentoring service for newly retired people. Steve loved exploring life and didn't need to live an extravagant lifestyle. There had been some lean times in between careers, and his family lived with the uncomfortable insecurity of not knowing where his next job would come from, but for the most part, Steve was genuinely happy in his work.

It seems like for most of us the first half of life is about exploring and finding out who we really are in the world of work. In the second half, there is an opportunity to clarify what we are good at and what kind of work we like to create the ideal job. Add in time and financial commitments to family and other nonwork pursuits, and hopefully we can create a winning career combination.

One career perspective that I like transcends job titles and compensation and focuses on leaving a legacy with your work. Often when you make a longer-lasting and broader contribution, you derive a deeper satisfaction in your work life. The legacy career focus is best captured by Buckminster Fuller's question: "What is it on this planet that needs doing, that I know something about, that probably won't happen unless I take responsibility for it?"

Reflecting on this question helps clarify who you want to be in the work world and leads to a sense of life purpose. That clarity becomes one of the points on your inner compass that allows you to make choices about how you want to spend your time and energy. With that sharpened discernment, you approach each day with a sense of purpose, courage, and urgency—as if your life depended on it. This becomes your calling.

A lifetime calling feels just right for who you are, is deeply satisfying, and fits like a glove. It's genuinely you and applies to situations both at the workplace and outside. Your calling transcends time and job titles and is broad enough to allow for many career reinventions. It serves as a reference when you make choices about how you want to spend your time or what activities you want to do. This clarity helps you stay centered and provides perspective when life seems chaotic or stressful. You're at your best, feel most empowered and passionate, when you're following your calling. It would be a perfect inscription for your gravestone.

People take different paths in defining their calling. Some individuals just know and have always known. Others methodically analyze, using career instruments and self-assessments to plot their career progression. Then, there are those who trust providence and fate to guide them in their life purpose. All processes can work, as long as you are deliberate about defining your calling and take it seriously.

My approach is to take an hour each day for a week, four times a year, and focus on the question I cited earlier. I write down my thoughts, ask trusted friends for their perspectives, and pay attention to intuitive insights. Sometimes my dreams provide help. Occasionally, a random encounter with a stranger, like someone I sit next to on a plane, has just the right perspective to add to my ongoing quest to answer my calling.

If you don't clarify your calling, you are doomed to be a victim of circumstance, habit, or someone else's calling. A clear sense of purpose leads to *full-powered presence*. When others know where you stand, you are less apt to be a target for those people who want to unduly influence or manipulate you. With your life purpose as one of your compass points, it is easier to take decisive action. People tend to gravitate towards those who are passionate about their purpose, and as leaders, they garner allegiance and respect.

It's important to realize that one's calling can appear in many shapes and sizes—not just in what we choose to do but also in how the message of that calling is delivered. Our task is not to question the delivery method used but to recognize that a deep transformation is occurring and then with courage act on the guidance that is given.

A powerful example is the following remarkable letter from *The Sun* magazine. It was written by Alison Clement.

"A guy I know was told by his doctor that he had cancer and would die in a year. There he was, working at a job that was OK but not great, living in a place that was nice but not paradise, dating a woman he liked a lot but didn't love. He was warming up, you know. The way most of us do.

"So what did he do? He quit his job, sold everything, packed up, and moved to Key West, where he bought a boat, because he always wanted to sail around the Keys in a little boat in the sunshine, and he did. After awhile, he went to see a doctor in Key West to see how much time he had left. The doctor got the guy's old records and ran new tests and then said the first doctor made a mistake: He'd never had cancer at all. I think about that guy sometimes, sailing around on his little boat in the ocean, living his dream, all because he found out he was mortal."

In aikido, it is important to be clear why you are practicing. Is your goal to increase your self-defense skills or raise your level of physical fitness? Are you interested in how the principles enhance your effectiveness off the mat or delighted in how aikido provides just the right activity to recharge after a tough day at work? Perhaps it's the friendships at the dojo or the meditative benefits of sword practice. Your clear purpose provides focus to your training and enhances your experience.

Irimi teaches us that choosing right action, with right timing and levels of power, requires we have a clear compass point from which to navigate. This compass point is essential to clearheaded leadership. The steps are simple. Go inward and look for all the guidance and signs you can to identify your calling. Finding your calling will require wisdom, patience, and discernment, and though challenging, it may be the easier part of the journey.

Then, once seen or felt, bring the same commitment you would on the mat—that is, bring every resource to bear—and make it happen. Begin to strip away all activity that is not essential to following your calling. Acting from that guidance and making your calling a reality in behavior and spirit will require the courage of a *randori* leader.

TRY THIS . . .

- Review your career path so far in your life and any ambitions that you have yet to achieve.

- What is unique about how you add value and make a difference?

- Are you maximizing your calling?

JH

GET
OFF THE MAT
THE SKILL
OF
DISENGAGEMENT

WHAT IS GET
OFF THE MAT?

The true test of character is . . . how we behave
when we don't know what to do.

—John Holt

Corporate America likes to think it only has two speeds:
fast and getting faster. Listen to the conversation in any business meeting, and you'll hear words like "reduce cycle time,"
"quicker customer response," "drive hard for results," and
"speed wins." Don't get us wrong. We see the benefit of
eliminating inefficient activity, so that customers have more
value. But we think most leaders have lost perspective and
now assume that pushing the throttle to full speed all the
time for all activities is the only path to get results. The mindset used to be "If in doubt, just do something . . . anything,
whether it's the best decision or not." Now it's "Just do lots
of things and fast." Leaders run the risk of losing their discernment about what activities really add value and forget
that one smart decision may be not to take action at all.

Consider the typical sword fight in Western and Eastern
cultures. Errol Flynn gets the honors as the master of Western swordplay, as he dramatically demonstrates in the mov-
ies. He is constantly dueling with his opponent, sparring up
and down the stairs, leaping on top of tables, and swinging
from drapery. Hundreds of times their swords clash, and several strikes draw blood but are rarely fatal. Exhilarating, yes.
Exhausting, absolutely. Eventually, just when it looks like he

is done for, the hero outwits with a last moment of superior strength to turn the defeat into victory.

Contrast that with what you may observe in an aikido sword match. Both partners simultaneously take one step back and draw their swords. Then they wait. There is no outer movement. Each person focuses his mind to be clear, free from fear and aggression. With that clarity and openness, each can tune into his partner, sensing any hesitation, anxiety, or rigidity in presence, all of which will create an opening for a deadly attack. Each is conserving vital energy, poised to move in one fully committed strike. Minutes pass. You might mistake them for two statues if you didn't pay attention to their intense concentration and feel the electricity emanating from the two partners, who know that only one sword strike will determine victory. Sometimes, the contest is decided in a flurry of *ki ai* shouts and a blur of sword movements that last maybe 30 seconds. More commonly, one person concedes defeat and respectfully bows to his partner, because he knows that to continue to attack would be fruitless or even deadly. The victor showed no openings in his mental state, emotional integrity, or physical readiness, and won through presence and not action.

Get off the mat is a term that describes the action of disengaging from a practice partner on the practice mat. Although most of the time aikidoists are careful in their practice, occasionally there is a situation that requires a halt in the action. For instance, one might be taking out "a bad day at the office" on his partner with overly aggressive attacks. Or, a novice student may be responding more vigorously than his partner can handle. Sometimes, two people get competitive and lose sight of the need for mutual respect. In those situations, to continue a style of practicing that can result in injury or a contentious relationship requires that both partners stop and make necessary changes. If one partner won't cease the inappropriate behavior, then the other disengages and literally steps off the practice mat.

Get off the mat in the business world is a tactic that is appropriate in a number of situations. One such occasion to consider is similar to the swordplay example when no action is the best choice. This is different from hesitating or procrastinating when the choice is clear. Instead, *get off the mat* or temporarily suspending activity in a project is appropriate when action would unnecessarily drain vital energy or the path is not clear. Ever have a Murphy's Law day when anything that can go wrong, does go wrong? Persisting through adversity is important, but sometimes it makes sense to suspend activity until the energy changes.

Get off the mat is also a clear choice to disengage from an interaction that may create harm or degenerate into a power struggle. To disengage is to firmly acknowledge the integrity of both people, the need for mutual respect, and the importance of right timing and approach. Different from retreating or giving in, *get off the mat* requires courage and bold action, leaving no room for your opponent to consider escalating the attack. By boldly disengaging, you send the message that you have clear expectations for appropriate behavior. You would rather cease activity than collude with an interaction that puts the relationship at risk or siphons off vital energy.

Get off the mat can also be appropriate when you are not at *full-powered presence*. Sometimes you need a break in activity to recenter and gain perspective or recharge your batteries. To continue interacting puts you at risk of making poor decisions or creating an opening for an "attack" from a colleague. It is better to be proactive in managing the state of your presence than to realize too late that you have compromised your position or made a wrong choice. It's another way to "go slow to go fast."

Finally, *get off the mat* complements *irimi* and *tenkan*. The choice to disengage is best made from a state of *full-powered presence*. It gives you the freedom to appropriately determine whether the situation would best be served with an *irimi* or *tenkan* approach, without feeling that you have to use one or the other. If in doubt, *get off the mat,* even if it's only for a few minutes, and allow the right approach to emerge. *Get off the mat* is the perfect antidote for our culture's addition to action and should be in the repertoire of every competent leader.

JH

OUR FEARS ARE ALWAYS STRONGEST BEFORE WE LET GO

Courage is the power to let go of the familiar.
—Raymond Lindquist

Recently, I had a conversation with a long-term client. She is the CEO of a managed care company in the South that specializes in Medicaid. This is not exactly a "sexy" business, but the company does great work. Essentially, her company provides health care services for low-income or needy individuals. It's an important and valuable mission.

My client had been extraordinarily successful in the four years of her tenure. When she started in this organization, it was losing money hand over fist. The company was literally hemorrhaging cash. Its problem was that it was jointly owned by seven regional hospitals. Their separate missions compelled them to take care of the poor, and this was their way of sharing the pain. As a board, they spent their time bickering and complaining about financial loss but with no way of resolving the issue. They lacked both the commitment and know-how to fix the problem. The organization was in a yearly downward spiral with a demoralized workforce. The picture was not pretty.

Enter Fran. In her first year as CEO, she stabilized the business and started to create a sense of optimism in the employees. By year three, the bottom line showed a healthy profit. In her tenure's fourth year, the swing from deficit to profit was $25 million—a big deal for a small managed care concern. Every other company of its kind in the state was losing money.

Given her success, you would think the board would have been overjoyed. They were not. An incredibly dysfunctional group, they spent more time arguing over territory than supporting the progress of the organization. Their behavior was shameless. When her annual compensation discussion was once again shortsighted and petty, she knew it was time to leave. Our conversation, on the heels of this compensation fiasco, was a powerful lesson in the difference between disengagement and giving up.

"I've decided to leave," she calmly started. "I just feel I've done what I came to do and met my commitments, and I can leave knowing I made a difference. My instincts tell me I'm 90 percent correct in this decision. The remaining 10 percent is just fear of the unknown. I get no appreciation from the board, with the money being the least of it. I realize it's just time."

When did she know?

"The knowing was almost immediate. For four years, I have been deeply committed, through good times and bad. But last week it just hit me. I was shrinking inside. The board was no longer tolerable to work for. Even though I don't have a job waiting for me, my future seems brighter. I can no longer stay working in an organization that continues to demoralize my spirit. Period. And that as they say is that."

Our meeting ended with hugs and good wishes for a strong meeting with the board. It was the first time in nearly 20 years of working with CEOs that I was genuinely delighted for someone to quit.

I spoke with her a few days later, fully expecting to hear the good news of her conversation. I was surprised. As firm and resolute as she was the day we spoke, as she neared her critical meeting, her anxieties took hold.

"I'm having doubts," she confessed.

What happened?

"You know that 10 percent uncertainty I talked about? Well, it keeps running around my head with all the 'yes, buts,' and it's driving me crazy. I don't know what to do."

Didn't she trust her instincts, the 90 percent she was so sure of a few days before?

"Well, yes," she said. "But I keep waking in the middle of the night with all these doubts. What if I'm wrong? What if the board thinks it's tied to salary? What if the organization falls apart when I leave?"

This pattern of back and forth is typical regarding the ambivalence in *get off the mat*. It is important to remember an essential and critical notion: Our fears are always strongest right before we let go. Often, just when we have made the decision to change, when we are most resolute in our commitment, when our intuition tells us we are 90 percent there, our fears come back in force. They are in a deep survival mode. The status quo is literally fighting for its life. That is the good news in every fearful resistance. It's an announcement of impending change.

Get off the mat teaches us to recognize our fears right before change as a typical part of the process of letting go. Consider them, give them some airtime, but recognize them for what they truly are—the last, best fight of something that needs to go. The greater the change, the greater the fight. All manner of demon may emerge, trying every type of psychological trick to dissuade us from our new course of action. The mind is infinite in its ability to sabotage our efforts at *get off the mat*.

Don't indulge your fear by acquiescing to its power. If you truly feel you are 90 percent there (and sometimes 51 percent is enough), then take the leap. Trust your instincts and the thoughtful process you have used to date. It is probably right. As D.H. Lawrence once said: "When one jumps over the edge, one is bound to land somewhere."

After a conversation about her fears, my client came to realize they were not as important as her future dreams. She handed in her resignation a week later. She has never been happier.

TRY THIS . . .

- Consider something or someone you are trying to let go of.

- Spend some time listing the fears that prevent you from acting.

- Then, set a timetable for making a decision, burn your list, and come hell or high water take action.

DB

RELATIONSHIPS AS A REASON, SEASON, OR LIFETIME

To every season, turn, turn, turn.

—The Old Testament

In learning when to *get off the mat* in relationships, it is sometimes helpful to consider the inherent quality of the relationship. Giving careful consideration to the nature of a relationship can help you decide whether to detach from the individual or continue to invest time and effort. One helpful way of understanding this inherent quality is to consider whether the relationship is a "reason," a "season," or a "lifetime" for you. When you figure out which one it is, the answer to how you approach this individual and the effort or detachment you bring will become clearer. In some cases, it will become obvious. It is a useful model for knowing when or when not to *get off the mat.*

Let's examine these three concepts.

The first is the possibility that someone is in your life for a reason. This typically means the nature of the relationship is based on a need you have or provides an important learning opportunity. The person is in your life to assist you through a difficulty, to provide you with guidance and support, or to aid you physically, emotionally, or spiritually. He or she may seem like a godsend at the time—and typically is! She is there for the *reason* you need them to be.

As is typical of this type of relationship, it suddenly becomes tenuous and frequently ends quickly and with lots of fireworks. The relationship becomes volatile usually without any wrongdoing on your part and often at an inconvenient time.

Sometimes, he or she will create unreasonable or unmanageable conflict. No matter what you say or do, nothing works. Her behavior literally forces you to take a stand and *get off the mat.* It's important to realize during these times that in essence your need has been met, and the purpose of the relationship has been fulfilled. And now it is time to move on. Your task is simple. Learn what you can, then let go. Step off. It's time.

The second possibility is that someone is in your life for a season. She oftentimes brings an experience of contentment, explosive creativity, or laughter. She may teach you how to do something you have never done. When you see this person, you become excited and animated, but the relationship will run its course over the term of a year or so and then seem to lose energy. It started out great with the promise that it would be a deep, long-term connection but then ended with a long, slow fizzle, like a balloon slowly but inevitably losing air deflates right in front of your eyes.

There is a tendency to dismiss either the importance of the connection or its value. Don't. Believe it! It is real! But its purpose was only for a season. Like a great meal that you savor, appreciate its lessons and learnings. Its value is to help for a period of time—longer than a reason, but not forever. But know that once the relationship has run its course, it's over.

Finally, lifetime relationships teach us lifetime lessons. This happens through an individual's presence or the gift of an essential message that will serve us for the rest of our lives. It gives us something solid on which to build our future integrity. A lifetime relationship is defined less by the daily company of the individual and more through either long-term connection to us or her essential message.

Think about Christmas cards. We have friends who we love all year even if the only time we think of them is at the holidays when we mail them a card.

Trust the nature of this relationship. There is something that cannot be articulated but sustains itself over time and distance—even if it's just through a simple message. Your job is to accept the person or the lesson and to honor the connection by doing only one thing: Put what you have learned to use in every other relationship and area in your life. Relationships are wise teachers for you. Don't squander the lifetime importance of their gift. Look for these teachers, even if they are only a one-sentence connection.

Years ago, I was trying to decide whether to divorce my first wife. It was a marriage I had been struggling in, and I needed to get out. I told my therapist I was going to tell my wife once I got past a few things.

"Like what?" she asked.

"I can't do it in October because it's her birthday," I explained. "November is Thanksgiving, so that's out. December is Christmas and New Year's—can't ruin her holiday. February we were supposed to go away for a vacation. I guess it will have to wait six months or so."

She slowly took my hand and compassionately said, "David, when you have to cut off a dog's tail, it's not less painful to the dog if you do it an inch at a time."

This is one sentence I have remembered all my life.

Get off the mat teaches us to consider carefully the nature of a relationship when it is problematic. Sometimes, we get in trouble by trying to extend a "reason" relationship into a "season" one or a "season" into a "lifetime." It's important to honestly assess the true nature of a relationship's inherent boundaries. Let that provide you with guidance on when or if to get off.

TRY THIS . . .

- Think of a few past relationships that ended with pain or unfinished business.

- View these relationships through the "reason, season, or lifetime" lens and see what, if anything, changes in your feelings.

- Or, consider the significant lifetime relationships you have and ask yourself, "Am I paying adequate attention to maintaining these relationships?"

DB

IF YOU'RE LOCKED INTO CONTROL, IT'S A GOOD IDEA TO GET OFF THE MAT

Trust is the softening of fear into awe.

—Lao-tzu

As psychologists know, most people have a powerful need to control and succeed. This need explains so much human behavior: work, relationships, war—all that stuff. A high degree of control helps us feel comfortable. A routine free from a lot of change feels familiar. It's what brings many of us solace.

The problem is that from a big-picture perspective, the pace of change has dramatically increased. Just look at the world around us. We live in such a complex age that no individual can ever direct the numerous situations that affect him or her daily. From the economy to the media to the government, change and sometimes chaos are constant. Consequently, some days it's a major accomplishment just to keep up, let alone feel like we are ahead of the wave.

This creates an interesting dilemma: How do we handle the discrepancy between what we want (control in our lives) and what we get (little or no control)?

One common response is to compensate by controlling the smaller aspects of our lives, the things over which we have some modicum of influence. If we can't control the major events, then we focus on smaller interactions. In a state of high change, this can mean some pretty small details in life.

When a leader gets out of balance, the tendency is to micromanage his direct reports. Projects get a little chaotic, and the manager wants to know more detail. External variables change, and the manager wants to make more decisions. When the organizational politics go a little haywire, the leader increases demands for update meetings. In the worst case, the leader sets the standard that he will never be surprised by any changes or decisions made by direct reports.

This increasingly high need for control means a death grip on your people. This micromanagement begins to look like requests for specificity in the extreme, asking for details not needed, or demanding unimportant information (to name a few). Direct reports feel undermined, second-guessed, and resentful of the added activity needed to make the boss feel comfortable.

The problem gets worse if the high need for control becomes a habit, because then we lose perspective on what is
really important. In fact, the intention of using high control
to get better results and maintain morale during change often
backfires. We'd like to suggest a different view, one shared by
Horsht Schultze, chairman of the Ritz Carlton Hotels.

Schultze once went to every department in every one of
his hotels and asked the following question: "How do you
want to be characterized a year from now?" Without exception, he got the same answer: "We want to be known as the
best." Knowing this, Schultze behaved accordingly by giving
autonomy and independence to his people. Rather than
increase control by getting more involved in day-to-day
business decisions, he did the opposite by giving every Ritz
employee a discretionary budget to improve customer satisfaction—no questions asked. They could spend the money
any way they wanted as long as it improved customer joy.

One key to letting go is to understand the dynamic between trust and control. They are opposite sides of the same
coin. Where we do not trust is inevitably where we will try
and overmanage a situation. It is that simple. In all relationships, whenever trust is low, this creates a vacuum that will be
filled with high control. Thus, if we want to let go of a situation, we need to examine where and why we do not trust the
parties and/or environment. Horsht Schultze chose to trust
that his employees would make the best decisions with their
money.

This notion creates an interesting paradox. What should
we do when the urge to control our environment is the very

same behavior that prevents us from trusting it in the first place?

On the aikido mat, when someone is overly controlling, he tends to get rigid and tight and less sensitive to the impact of his movements. In such a case, either one or both partners often sustain a minor injury. You would think that high control would prevent harm, but it is just the opposite. If someone can't step out of his or her high control attitude, it is best to leave the mat for that class.

The same standard should exist for leadership. When you feel under siege from a lot of chaos and your first instinct is to move into control, think *get off the mat* instead. Rather than create harm, disengage from the situation until you can return in more balanced *full-powered presence.*

Get off the mat teaches us to ask, "How can I increase my trust in outcome so I can let go? What's the best way to let my people do their best?" Then find a way to support them, and you will build their capability to manage chaos and their loyalty to you as leader.

TRY THIS . . .

- Trust is based on predictability. When we are left guessing in a relationship or situation, it's hard to trust.

- Consider a situation where your trust level is low.

- What can you do to increase predictability?

DB

GET OFF THE MAT
OF YOUR CALENDAR

In the fight between you and the real world, back the world.

—Frank Zappa

A colleague, Sandra Janoff, once told me, "Eighty percent of life's aggravation and stress is caused by scheduling." I have always tended to think she had a good point. Certainly, most of the grief and aggravation I deal with is usually *all about scheduling.* Who I see, when I see them, what I do, the choices I make or don't make are all about time, and time is all about scheduling.

I was considering Sandra's comment as I was one day boarding yet another plane—a plane three hours late and promising a long night. It felt like a classic situation for me. I took the late flight because I didn't want to upset my wife by leaving early. But because I took the late flight during the summer, it was typically delayed for bad weather. I ended up missing a client dinner, and consequently, a client who was going to a restaurant that I wasn't. I was deeply frustrated.

Thus, it was all the more remarkable I ended up sitting next to Kathy and Tom Super, from Washington, D.C. Kathy and Tom are a delightful couple who look to be in their early 50s. They have an air about them of relaxed friendliness and quiet confidence. This internal comfort was hard to miss as they boarded and sat down next to me.

As we took off, I started talking to them with the usual airplane banter.

"Going home?" I asked.

"Yes," Kathy responded.

"Where were you?" I continued.

"In Maine for the weekend," Tom quietly said.

"Where in Maine?" I kept asking.

"Kennebunkport. Visiting friends."

"Really," I chuckled. "George and Babs in?" I smirked, trying to be witty. Sheepishly they exchanged a quick glance, and Kathy said, "Well, *that's* who we were visiting."

Oh please. This was too good to be true. I *had* to continue now! "Do you mind if I ask you how you know President Bush?"

"No, go right ahead," Kathy politely responded. "He's my boss." At this point, all decorum was thrown to the wind.

"Your boss? What do you *do?*"

"I keep President Bush's calendar. For the last 11 years, I have been his scheduler. You know, set appointments, decide who sees him, that kind of thing."

I could not believe my ears. Here I was, in the middle of a self-imposed scheduling crisis, and I ended up sitting next to a woman who keeps the calendar for a former president of the United States—a man who at one point in his life was arguably the busiest and most powerful man on earth. When was I going to get another opportunity like *this?* How could I *not* ask for advice? Once I got the OK from Kathy, I started to fire away. Primarily, I asked for secrets on scheduling and what someone in a regular life should know to make her life easier.

Her answers were crisp and clear—what you would expect from someone who was totally confident based on years of success. Her advice was profound. Here's what Kathy told me.

"First," she started, "make sure you strike a balance between what's important versus what's urgent. You don't want to end up being a slave to the urgent unless it connects in some critical ways to the important. This is essential, so that you don't lose track of the big picture. A president's life can be taken up with all types of emergencies, so you must manage to a larger perspective—a bigger view. A calendar can get filled with so much nonsense. Usually, it has a tag on it that says "urgent." Be careful not to fall prey to *only* those demands. Focus on what matters and try not to waste a second.

"Secondly," she continued, "be careful about the assumptions that get created when you make commitments. Many times, constituents will consider a one-time meeting as an annual event. They will assume that because you do something once, it's a yearly occasion. For instance, a photo opportunity for muscular dystrophy can turn into an annual photo opportunity if you are not careful. It doesn't mean it's not important, but you may not be able to do it *every* year. It's critical to manage for the assumptions of others and be clear about the boundaries. Otherwise, four years into the term, you've got your schedule filled with obligations that have been building over time.

"Finally, learn to say no politely, so that you don't hurt people. For the president's standing appointments, I would schedule approximately 50 meetings a week in 15-minute slots. For those 50 weekly slots, we received about *1,000 requests!* I had a staff of 11 whose job was basically to sort through the invites and kindly decline. We had 62 different letters that would go out depending on the request. We would get everything from mall openings to worried mothers wanting guidance for their daughters—but the goal was always the same. Don't hurt people. Do it nicely, politely, and kindly. *No* may be one of the most important words a president can learn."

My flight ended with Kathy and Tom as it started—easily and with warm handshakes. What is clear is that Kathy is a *get off the mat* master when it comes to scheduling. For us mere mortals, grappling with our calendars, she has a wise and powerful message—if we listen.

TRY THIS . . .

- An important way to get off the calendar mat is to learn to say no.

- Be ruthless. Remove yourself from 5 to 10 percent of your standing meetings.

- If you think you can't, ask your staff to make some recommendations. They'll give you 20 percent.

DB

LEAD FROM THE SHADOWS

The good and the wise lead quiet lives.

—Euripides

Most of the time, a manager needs to be directly involved with the important projects, visible to the team, and provide hands-on leadership. Even with highly capable direct reports, a leader needs to be seen as an advocate, a backup set of hands in a crisis, and a provider of moral support. Too often, managers fail to strike that balance, either getting overinvolved in the details of projects or swinging to the opposite extreme and disappearing. You'd be surprised how many of our clients tell us that they haven't had a substantial conversation with their boss for months.

The fast pace of business creates a polarity of options: either be direct, face-to-face, and hands-on as a manager *or* completely delegate and virtually disappear. We think the right combination is do both: closely supervise when appropriate, delegate with sufficient support at other times, *and* employ a third approach, which is leading from behind the shadows.

I had an interesting experience while being attacked by four of my colleagues during a *randori* practice. My sensei suggested that one strategy to deal with multiple attackers was to seek the open spaces away from everyone. If my attackers converge into the middle, move towards the far, open corner. Focus less on direct engagement and instead use the open space to diffuse the challenges.

Because I was used to staying in the thick of things, walking away from the action felt like I was quitting. But I decided to give it a try. During the first attack, I moved to an open space near the edge of the mat, thus avoiding confrontation. Again, my attackers approached, and I again tried the same tactic—this time moving back to the middle. I was keenly aware of my adversaries, but my focus changed from standing my ground to seeking the shadows. My attackers weren't any less committed, but their energy began to shift from "let's get this guy" to "where is he going next?" While dissipating the focused attacks, their perspective expanded. By drawing them away from the center and into the open spaces, out of the attack spotlight and into the shadows, they inadvertently shifted from an aggressive mindset to a more collaborative and playful one. The result was a very dynamic, invigorating practice, full of surprises—my best *randori* performance so far.

Leading from behind the shadows in the workplace asks the manager to think about how he or she can support the success of direct reports *from behind the scenes.*

Here are a few examples of what we mean: A team member who just hit a home run with a project gets a nice letter from the CEO, prompted by you.

After two direct reports go home exhausted from trying to debug a software problem, you spend a few extra hours that night and leave the solution on their desks, for them to take credit for later on with the team.

You suggest to your direct report that she, instead of you, do the presentation of a successful departmental result to senior management.

Resources for a project show up without a lot of fanfare.

No doubt about it, probably 80 percent of leadership needs a direct approach. Employees need to know you are clearly in charge and visibly linked with your actions. But selectively leading from behind the scenes positively impacts a team in some subtle, but powerful ways. A message is sent that even if not present, you are still in touch with your team.

Out of sight, however, does not mean out of mind. You don't want your team to feel abandoned or anxious but instead more productive. Your direct reports will begin to develop some curiosity about what helpful action you'll take next, almost creating an "elf" effect. Most important, a contagious effect may set in where team members start helping each other also from behind the scenes.

Get off the mat teaches us that the highest form of leadership is taking positive action anonymously. While difficult to do in a closely situated team environment, if you pay attention, you'll begin to find more and more opportunities. Your direct reports do need to know where they stand with you, what results meet your expectations, and where their strengths are—straight from the horse's mouth. They also need to see visible examples of your support, garnering resources for their projects and advocating for them with senior management. But it deepens loyalty and adds some surprise and enjoyment to the normal intensity of corporate life to occasionally lead from behind the shadows.

Remember the words of Lao-tzu: "True leaders are hardly known to their followers . . . when the work's done, with no fuss or boasting, ordinary people say 'Oh, we did it.'"

TRY THIS . . .

- Select a direct report, colleague, or friend.

- For one month, provide anonymous support that enables her to meet her goals.

JH

DISENGAGEMENT: THE ART OF TAKING NO ACTION

Try? There is no try. There is only do or do not do.

—Yoda in *The Empire Strikes Back*

We Americans are addicted to activity—multitasking, double-booking meetings, and checking voice mail while playing Uno with the kids and tuning into CNBC in the background. God forbid we lose our Palm Pilots. This bias for action has its pluses. Innovative solutions come from trial and error, quick initiative gives market advantage to the early entrants, and bosses feel more comfortable when their direct reports look busy. What has been lost is the judgment of when to take action and *when not to.*

The path of effortless leadership assumes that there will be times to take appropriate action and other times to shift to neutral. Taking your foot off the gas can be important to wait for better timing, to conserve resources, or to be patient for the right course of action to become clear. Perhaps a team is not fully prepared or the right combination of business partners has not been formed to create the most powerful alliance. Sometimes, disengagement takes more courage, particularly if there is momentum in the organization to take action. It requires both patience to wait and decisiveness to shift gears when the time is right.

Taking no action is a deliberate decision and requires boldness. It is not the same as procrastination, which is the hesitancy to move forward, usually based in fear. Nor is disengagement similar to giving up. There is no defeat in taking no action, no loss of respect for disengagement. Delaying a decision by sending it to a committee for further study when the choice is clear is not what we're talking about. Nor is refusing to participate because you don't like the decision. That's a passive-aggressive tactic.

On the mat, you will disengage or choose to take no action for a number of reasons. For one, because *full-powered presence* is the cornerstone of the *randori principles,* you won't step on the mat until you are ready. You can tell how ready someone is by the quality of his bow. If your partner has a haphazard or casual bow, you know he is not paying full attention. Also, you may take a break if a series of attacks has thrown you off balance. To continue receiving attacks when you are off center or underpowered puts you in a risky position. It's not uncommon for *uke,* the person providing the attack, to stop midstream, because he senses you are not fully present and can get hurt.

Another reason to disengage on the mat is if you are overextended from fatigue or need time to integrate the lessons. Sometimes, it makes sense to step off the mat and watch some of the class. Seeing the techniques performed by your colleagues may give you a different perspective. I use this tactic when I've tried numerous times to perform a new movement and I just can't get it. Taking a break to recharge after a vigorous practice is also demonstrating responsibility for your own resources, and not overextending yourself to the point of injury.

Still another opportunity for disengagement is when the intention of your practice partner is not one of mutual respect and collaboration. On rare occasions, someone will have difficulty keeping a bad day at the office off the mat. Or, a "young buck" will be feeling his oats and end up using more power than necessary to neutralize the attack. Maybe a colleague will be inclined to take out his frustrations on a partner. Sensing the energy and the attitude of another aikidoist is important, and if you feel there is a hint of questionable intention, it is important to stop the practice and make clear your concerns. Most of the time, colleagues appreciate the feedback and make appropriate adjustments. Otherwise, it's time to disengage and find another practice partner.

In the workplace, leaders need to be able to discern those opportunities for disengagement or taking no action. Both are important tactics on the path to effortless leadership. Ask yourself these questions:

- What is the overall energy level of my team? At what point do I need to stop the activity level long enough for them to recharge?

- Rather than saying yes to all requests, can I build in downtime for my team so that we can conserve vital energy critically needed for the next big project?

- If my team members, in spite of best intentions, can't focus on the meeting agenda because of legitimate distractions, do I take action to cancel the meeting?

- What business opportunities have not evolved enough that it would be better to wait before committing resources and taking action?

- Am I willing to end a conversation if the other person is disrespectful and not willing to collaborate?

- Do I know my direct reports well enough to tell the difference between when they are appropriately taking no action and procrastinating?

- Can I decisively lead in a state of no action, making it clear to my team why we are taking this approach and not siphoning off vital energy in busywork?

- Do I only reward "doers" or do I instead value both the accomplishment of results and the conservation of team resources for the long term?

Disengaging and the art of taking no action require boldness and decisiveness and are important components of the path of effortless leadership. Habitually staying in high gear and indiscriminately throwing activity towards business goals create lack of focus and misuse of resources on a team. Knowing when to wait and carefully guarding the capacity of an organization can have huge strategic advantage. Setting high standards of behavior and disengagement from any disrespectful or harmful interaction protects the team and builds trust in the leader. In the stillness, victory can be achieved.

TRY THIS . . .

- Consider a project where it would be wise to temporarily suspend all activity.

- Then, deliberately take no action as a viable leadership choice.

JH

UNPLUG FROM POWER STRUGGLES

The supreme challenge of a warrior is to turn an enemy's
fearful wrath into harmless laughter.

—John Stevens

Sometimes your multiple attack practice doesn't go well. I'm not talking about a strike that hits its mark because your timing was late. Or maybe you took too long to neutralize one attack, creating an open target for that adversary coming in just off your right shoulder. These situations are part of the *randori* territory and provide valuable learning. You bow to your partners and thank them for pointing out, through their committed attacks, how your timing was off or that you were narrowly focused in your response. Then start fresh with the next round.

Sometimes, however, a respectful *randori* practice can degenerate into a struggle and become as close to a street fight as you can have in an aikido dojo. It doesn't take much for damage to occur once the downward spiral starts. Maybe attackers have shifted from clear, committed attacks to a competitive "let's get 'em" attitude. Initially playful, their intention changes to trying to defeat or embarrass their partners. At the last second, they may change their attack or pull back on the strike, making it difficult to respond. The attackers resist being thrown and end up grappling. The scene quickly resembles a rugby scrum.

The *nage,* or person being attacked, can also trigger this mayhem. If he or she is focused on looking good or not being embarrassed, she will become tight and less responsive. Such a person may use too much power in an effort to just finish off the attackers and "get the craziness over with quickly." Rushing and using too much force will trigger a revenge attitude in attackers and will escalate the speed and intensity of their strikes. Now, the *nage* is both anxious about looking bad and fearful about the increased level of attacks. As a result, he or she will either try one last valiant stand or cave under the pressure.

The result is always the same. A highly respectful practice quickly degenerates into a win-lose power struggle. Someone may be injured. Feelings are hurt, trust shattered, and finger pointing results. "Why did you have to crush me with your throw?" "I wouldn't have if you had just given me a straight attack." Back and forth they trade hurtful barbs until the sensei has to step in to mediate. A dark cloud of ill will permeates the practice mat. At that moment, it's critical for these colleagues to genuinely apologize to each other, acknowledge their responsibility as well as what they learned, and renew their commitment to practice in a respectful manner. Otherwise, they run the risk of becoming real adversaries, doubting each other's intentions and wary to even step onto the mat together.

Angeles Arrien has done some important research into the nature of power struggles. She points out that, often based in fear or pride, power struggles will only result in someone losing, exhausting vital energy, and doing irreparable harm. On the mat, a sensei keeps a keen eye aware for these dangerous situations, because once started, power struggles degenerate quickly, people get hurt, and the respectful morale of the school is suddenly at risk. Students who instigate a power struggle on the mat more than once are often dismissed from the dojo.

The same dynamics are at play in the business world, and leaders need to be both aware of the dynamics of power struggles and willing to take bold action to address them.

On the mat, the first tactic in diffusing a power struggle is to immediately stop the practice and state your concern or request: "You are pulling your energy out of your attack at the last moment. Please give me a fully committed strike, so I have something to work with." Or, "Your throw had more force to it than was needed. Please throttle back on your power." It's important to be clear about your feedback and to stop the action before the power struggle gains momentum.

Leaders need to look for the symptoms of power struggles and address them early on before any damage occurs. Look for interactions where the focus has shifted away from the business problem towards two colleagues prolonging the discussion just to win the argument. Pay attention to dynamics where two individuals trade barbs any chance they can. Or be aware of situations where the focus is on who gets the last word. Has the playful competitive tone of the team degenerated into a win-lose, cut-throat environment?

Bold, decisive action is needed to diffuse a power struggle. A leader needs to call a stop to the behavior and get at the root of the disagreement. Sometimes two individuals are just having a bad day. But if the leader typically responds to power struggles with denial and hopes that they will just go away, she runs the risk of the struggles escalating to a level that will be twice as hard to neutralize. Power struggles can have a life of their own, transcending the specific individuals involved, and need to be addressed immediately.

On the mat, if stopping the interaction and making specific requests doesn't work, the next tactic is to step away from the practice altogether. "This is starting to be dangerous, and I don't want anybody to get hurt. Let me know when you can be more respectful in your attacks." Or, "I'm having an off day and can't seem to break my habit of using too much force. Let's take a break and try the *randori* practice later on." In each case, a premium is placed on maintaining a respectful and vibrant practice rather than risk a power struggle taking root and someone getting hurt.

The same applies for leaders in the workplace. If your colleagues don't respond to your requests for more collaborative behavior, then you need to disengage from the interaction. This may mean stopping a conversation or ending a meeting. It may result in separating two team members who run the risk of pulling the whole project into a power struggle. Disengaging may take the form of not colluding with your boss who is unknowingly, or unfortunately deliberately, setting up a harmful competition between colleagues.

Power struggles don't just go away. If left unaddressed, power struggles will create irreparable harm, exhaust vital energy in a team that could be more productively applied elsewhere, and disrupt the path of effortless leadership. You need to take *irimi*-style action to disrupt the dangerous pattern.

Finally, power struggles are only diffused when all parties involved take individual responsibility for their own actions, make a genuine apology, and recommit to a respectful standard of interaction. Sometimes, it only takes one bold action like decisively ending a meeting midstream to get people's attention, so that they can return to more appropriate behavior. In other cases, disengaging and then making clear requests are important, so that your business colleagues understand that what is important resolves the conflict. In more entrenched power struggles, you need to stay disengaged until your partners change their behavior. In those cases, getting *off the mat* is the only effective leadership approach.

TRY THIS . . .

- Review the symptoms of a power struggle.

- Are you participating in any at the moment?

- If so, take decisive action by establishing a "cooling down" period, so you can disengage before irreparable harm is done.

JH

LET GO OF WHAT YOU CREATE

Do your work, then step back . . .
He who clings to his work will create nothing that endures.
If you want to accord with the Tao, just do your job, then let go.
—Tao Te Ching

Recently, our small town of Peterborough, New Hampshire, hosted ten Tibetan monks from the Drepung Gomang monastery in India. They were traveling in the United States for a year on a fund-raising tour. They came to Peterborough to create a visual prayer of compassion called a sand mandala. *Mandala* means sacred circle, and it is a way of creating a pattern that represents one's prayers and devotions. Many cultures around the world use them for focus and prayer. There are mandalas of many sorts, but the Tibetan mandalas are known for their incredible beauty and attention to time-honored detail. Watching the monks work was one of the great experiences of my life.

Every day, they would start with a half hour of prayer and chanting. Then, silently, the monks would start to work on the floor, four at a time, creating this extraordinary work of art and devotion. Using ancient patterns and techniques, the mandala created was a four-foot by four-foot masterpiece. With nothing but crushed colored marble and a few old funnels, it became an inspiration to almost everyone who saw it.

The level of detail was almost inconceivable: Tiny deer with even tinier eyes, small identical trees with minute leaves, mirrored patterns of such complexity they were hard to track because they were matched throughout the mandala in contrasting colors. Adults and children alike were drawn in openmouthed amazement at what they were seeing. It was spectacular.

At the end of the five days, a ceremony was held to honor the spirit of the work. The small building in which the mandala was created was packed. The monks in full ceremonial garb sang, chanted, and played huge, loud horns. Then, the head monk calmly stood, prayed over this magnificent work, and proceeded to calmly draw a ceremonial knife through its four directions. Then with a matter-of-fact deliberateness, the remaining monks began to brush their work into a glass jar. The sand was to be released into the town river. When the dismantling ceremony began, I actually heard the crowd gasp, but the monks proceeded with no emotion, no attachments, and no discernible sense of loss. Some people even cried in amazement. The sweeping lasted no more than two minutes, which stood in sharp contrast to the five days it took to create the mandala.

This level of detachment is a powerful ancient model to consider in a world where the new catchphrase is "built to last." Instead, ask yourself, "Where can I detach from that which has run its course?" This is different from being open to outcome in an interaction. We are talking instead about letting go of a product or process that, for whatever reason, has served its purpose.

Our friend Tricia Burt is an accomplished artist. She told me that during her early classroom training, she was asked to create a new painting every day. Then at the end of every session the entire class would paint over their work and start again fresh. Sometimes it killed her. But in retrospect, she said it was one of her most powerful lessons as an artist. The message was clear. To be fully and totally creative means letting go of the past—and that includes even one's accomplishments when they no longer serve.

This does not mean that you must see everything as impermanent. After all, most of us are not Buddhist monks or painters. We get rewarded for creating change that has sustainability. But, there is something in this thinking that can be helpful to leaders in getting off the mat of that which no longer works in the bigger picture.

In aikido, for example, you may spend two years at a dojo learning a particular style and earning a relatively high level of skill. Then you go to your first national conference. On the mat with a partner from a different school in a different part of the country, you are asked to attack and defend a particular move. He or she may have learned it differently. If you resist his form because you are attached to your dojo's way of doing things, you will inevitably create unnecessary tensions.

It is the same in business. Attachment to something that works today may close you off from finding something even better tomorrow.

One of our clients is an IT vice president for a successful financial services company. She is also ultimately in charge of the help desk. Typically, the IT help desk in any organization is the job from hell. It is characterized by nothing but complaints from frustrated and angry users. The employee base usually suffers from horrendous turnover balanced by a few long-term employees who tend to be a bit eccentric and have high thresholds for customer complaints. This was the picture when our client took over.

She made the help desk one of her highest priorities. In two years, she completely transformed it into a model of stability and customer responsiveness. Team members cross-trained in each other's skills and gradually developed into a close-knit group. Turnover dropped and results significantly improved

A few years later, the company reorganized. The change moved the organization from a model of centralization to one of regional remote operations. For our client, this required a very difficult choice point. The right decision was to disband the team with appreciation and gratitude rather than keep a structure that no longer reflected the company's new direction. But she was very attached to something she had successfully created and was doing quite well.

Initially, she fought the change. And truth be told, she could have made it work. But she knew it wasn't right, as she began to see the inevitable implications of possible future tension points. In a moment of great leadership, she dismantled what she had so wonderfully built.

As a leader, the lesson is profound. Every product, strategy, process, and/or cash cow has an inevitable end date. Detachment, once past appropriateness, is one of your hardest decisions as a leader. This means making sure that for every significant function or product in your domain, you have a clear answer for the following question: "What is the purpose this serves?" When it stops fulfilling its purpose, no matter how successful it has been, bow inwardly in gratitude and get off the mat.

Remember the wise words of organizational consultant Harrison Owen, who said, "When it's over, it's over!"

TRY THIS . . .

- Make a list of your five most productive services or product lines.

- Consider under what circumstances and why you would end them.

- Have this discussion with your team and request they periodically ask, "Is it time and, if not, why?"

MOVING TO ADVANCED RANDORI

MASTERING LEADERSHIP

THE DANCE OF
ADVANCED RANDORI
LEADERSHIP

A master uses 90 percent intuition and 10 percent technique.

—O'Sensei

Once you understand each of the basic skills of the *randori principles,* you can begin to integrate them in more challenging situations. The blending of the turning and connecting of *tenkan* sets up the opportunity for a perfectly timed *irimi* tactic. *Full-powered presence* gives you the perspective to choose to diffuse resistant energy from a colleague or *get off the mat* by disengaging from the conversation. An adversary, sensing your readiness to use *irimi,* may shift her intention and welcome a *tenkan* gesture of joint ownership. The willingness to *get off the mat* will often neutralize an overly aggressive conversation style.

Each of the four *randori* skills has merit on its own, and the integration gives increased power and effectiveness. In making the choices of how to integrate, an effective leader needs to expand her ability to read colleagues while instantly applying the right approach. By being unattached to how an interaction will evolve, and ready to instantly change tactics if needed, a leader maintains an effective and balanced approach to the ongoing flow of challenges. Eventually, this integrative process becomes intuitive and effortless.

At the advanced *randori* level, a leader places a premium on focusing on and returning quickly to *full-powered presence,* because it is from that foundation that the best judgments about approach, timing, and power can be made. *Full-powered presence* becomes second nature, and the awareness of the intention, energy, and responsiveness of a colleague becomes finely tuned. At this level, change is not perceived as a positive or negative event. It just is, and the challenge to the leader is to quickly read the situation and make the right move. Sometimes this is *irimi,* sometimes it is *tenkan,* and sometimes you even *get off the mat.* Whatever action choice is made, a premium is placed on diffusing resistance, preventing struggle, and finding the effortless path.

Effortless leadership is rarely an either/or proposition. Instead, like an improvisational dance, one moves between *irimi* and *tenkan,* centering with *full-powered presence* while always keeping a larger *randori* perspective. The different styles when used in consort leverage the benefits of each, creating a larger and more powerful impact.

Advanced *randori* means as a leader you always look for the flow of potential openings to create movement in an effortless fashion. Like a line of dominoes, one action can lead to another, creating a fast and powerful impact.

Remember, to be advanced as a leader means feeling comfortable using all styles and letting the situation, rather than your personal comfort with any one technique, dictate the choices you make.

The following chapters will give you a feel for how this "flow" might look.

JH

DEVELOP A WARRIOR'S SOUL

Start where you are, use what you've got, do what you can.

—Arthur Ashe (when asked how to be great)

A favorite fable is told that takes place in feudal Japan. One day a soldier guarding a road stops an old Buddhist priest. The soldier threateningly draws his sword and with challenge says to the priest, "Who are you? Where are you going? Why are you going there?"

The priest quietly thinks for a moment and gently says, "May I ask you a question?"

"Go ahead," the soldier belligerently responds.

"How much does the Shogun pay you a week?"

"Two baskets of rice."

"I will pay you four baskets of rice if you promise to ask me those questions every day."

I *love* this story, for within it rests the soul of a warrior.

Ultimately, this book is not just about leadership; it is also about warriorhood. And, if you want to be a great warrior (and there are many in the business world), it is important to understand what constitutes the warrior mindset and how you make choices as a leader.

The most important thing to remember is that warriors tend to follow a deeper, inner creed or guidance. They make decisions according to their internal compass. This is not to say that honor, duty, and loyalty do not play a part in their personal creed, but following orders is not all that dictates their decisions and actions.

Warriors are *not* typically followers. Rarely are they so tied to their organization's power structure that they will blindly support that structure if it goes against their own internal creed. Instead, their personal beliefs and values impact how they operate in the world. This does not mean that warriors reject out of hand something that they disagree with. They always respectfully voice their differences and act from integrity when doing something challenging to their creed. If they are leaders, they bring that creed forward with expectations for their team.

For instance, Jack Welch at GE had a model he used for all his top people of a four-box window that measured the two variables of values and performance. He was very clear. It was not enough to just be a high performer. You also had to exhibit behaviors that placed you high on the values quadrant. If you couldn't place high in both areas, you were not a member of his team. Period.

Another important point is that warriors typically do not see the enemy as *external,* as a force to be dehumanized and attacked. "Gooks," "Krauts," "Japs," "Slopes" are all historical attempts at diminishing the humanity of an opposing force. Nonwarriors will turn the enemy into someone or something to which they cannot relate. But a warrior rarely dehumanizes an opponent. A warrior, for instance, would never stoop to name calling or derogatory slang characterizations of the opposing force. Even the term *enemy* seems to hold little value.

Regardless of strength or power differences, the opposition is considered "worthy." It is what sits behind the ceremonial bow in an aikido match. Always, no matter what, hold your opponent in the highest esteem, because honor does not come just from winning but from the honor one conveys to others.

This means that a warrior understands the biggest battle is not with an external force, but resides within. The biggest enemy for a warrior is the "shadow," a psychological term that means his own inner demons, neuroses, or dysfunctional patterns. The shadow is our internal power struggle with ourselves, the battle we all face every day between those inner forces that either support or diminish our human spirit.

A nonwarrior will sometimes turn the shadow into an external enemy, but the warrior knows it resides within. An unacknowledged shadow, when combined with opportunity, will always lead to the irresponsible abuse of power.

The implication of this difference is profound.

To be a warrior means a willingness to consistently look within and ask how one's personal demons impact actions and decisions. It means continually wrestling with the tougher, inner issues that confront our external realities. Clashes of ego, power struggles with others, bouts of insecurity, lashing out at subordinates, a continued sense of depression—these are all signs of an unacknowledged or poorly managed shadow. It means you are drifting away from warriorhood.

When that battle is ignored, and it frequently is by even the most powerful of leaders, then "mischief" of the most destructive kind finds its way into organizational life. The

228

Wall Street Journal is filled almost weekly with stories of abusive forms of power that would make your hair curl. Remember "Chainsaw" Al Dunlop? Sadly, nonwarriors, no matter what organizational rank, are much easier to find then warriors.

TRY THIS . . .

- For one year, ask yourself every day the following three questions: "Who am I?" "Where am I going?" and "Why am I going there?"

- Then take one minute every day to remind yourself that an organization is not an honorable place to play out personal issues.

- Do this for one year and note how profound are the differences in your warrior soul.

DB

LEADER AS WORTHY ADVERSARY

Don't goof off.

—Suzuki Roshi

In my opinion, one of the highest compliments you can give someone in aikido is the accolade of worthy adversary. I have been very fortunate to practice with many wonderful people over the years, and from each one I benefited. Some were high-ranking Black Belts with knowledge of thousands of techniques. Others were beginners asking questions from a different perspective and giving me new insights on the art. Still others were just plain fun to practice with. But the worthy adversaries were the most memorable. They offered something unique and rare, just like those few leaders you would follow in a moment's notice.

What makes a worthy adversary so special? Here are the key components, by way of aikido illustration and then with application to leadership.

First, the ability to focus is extraordinary. Consider my friend Toby. Outside the aikido class, she was as sociable and friendly as anyone, but as soon as she stepped on the mat, she was intensely serious about her practice. Toby did not dilute her concentration with extraneous conversation or casual participation. Year after year, she gave each class 100 percent of her effort. I always knew that when I practiced with Toby, it was time to take the art of aikido very seriously.

Worthy adversaries in business can discern what's most essential and treat work activities with the maximum seriousness. They know how to create an environment where priorities are clear and remove distractions so their team members can focus. These leaders are explicit with their expectations and don't tolerate a halfhearted, casual approach to important work. "Work hard, play hard" is clearly understood.

Second, I would add the quality of unrelenting commitment to help others be their best. My friend and teacher Chris always pushed me at just the next level of my capabilities. With only a moment to bask in the glory of my last improvement, I had to continually refocus to handle the next attack. He would bring me right to the edge of my skill but not cross the line of shaking my self-confidence. Chris helped me keep pride at bay and, in the process, avoid slipping into arrogance or worse stop learning.

Worthy adversaries are unrelenting in expecting the best of their people. They get to know the capabilities of their people and know how to stretch them to the next level. These leaders also pay close attention to their direct reports and notice when individuals start to go offtrack. When direct reports know they can't get away with subpar performance, they hold themselves accountable for higher levels of performance. By carefully and continuously raising the bar, these leaders expand the capability of the team without putting their confidence at risk.

Third, when I practiced with Sensei Richard Moon, I got instant and honest feedback about my technique. If I was too rigid in my attack, he would deliver a tough countertechnique. And if I took a hard fall to the mat (my fault for being too rigid), he didn't let up—no apologizing or accommodating. If my *irimi* technique was halfhearted, Richard would not be thrown just to make me look good. Sure, he would point out alternatives if I asked, but if I didn't change my technique, he didn't back off in his response. He did this without fail over and over again.

Leaders as worthy adversaries let their colleagues know where they stand in a direct and honest way. Although empathetic when projects get offtrack, they don't tolerate excuses

MOVING TO ADVANCED RANDORI **231**

or collude with the illusion that everything's OK, both of which are considered forms of disrespect to a worthy adversary. These leaders are honest and tactful in keeping important business issues on the table and persistently guard against any behavior that undermines the truth.

Fourth, Ruth demonstrated the unselfishness and compassionate qualities of a worthy adversary. She consistently tuned into everyone on the mat. If someone was struggling, she would put her own practice aside to offer assistance. She respected what her colleagues wanted and provided the assistance they needed, both on the mat and off. Without a lot of fanfare, she quietly took care of things in just the right way—nothing more, nothing less. She was instrumental in creating a tone of compassion and respect at the aikido school, elevating the level of trust.

Leaders who combine unrelenting accountability with compassion are worthy adversaries. They feel deeply for their direct reports but don't overly caretake. These leaders respect what direct reports say they need, rather than make their own assumptions. They are seen as available and reliable and able to provide support that allows recipients to save face.

Sensei Steve Kalil models the fifth quality of a worthy adversary, because he demonstrates uncommon humility and gratitude. Even though he has been teaching for over 15 years and is highly ranked, Steve welcomes new techniques that students may bring from other dojos. Other teachers may arrogantly dismiss these different approaches. He has missed only a handful of classes and received very little compensation for his dedication to the aikido dojo. "I have so much to be grateful for. Teaching is a small way for me to re-turn the many gifts I have received from aikido," is his usual response. He strongly influences the positive tone on the mat, one of learning, dedication, and humility.

Worthy adversaries are quick to accept responsibility when things don't go well. They take responsibility for their actions and apologize fully if appropriate. These leaders don't dwell on their mistakes, but learn from them, and then move on. In spite of their skill, worthy adversaries don't allow pride to create an environment of elitism and compet-itiveness, where blind spots may underestimate a colleague. Worthy adversaries are genuine and forthright in expressing gratitude.

Worthy adversaries have these combinations of traits: concentration, dedication to colleagues, unrelenting honesty, compassion, and humility and gratitude. When leaders incor-porate these characteristics with the *randori* approaches, they then develop teams that are consistently at their best and achieve effortless results.

TRY THIS . . .

- Are you a worthy adversary as a leader and in your personal life?

- Ask three colleagues or friends to give you feedback on the degree to which you are unrelenting in your focus, high standards, humility, and honesty with others.

JH

EFFORTLESS AND SUSTAINABLE

The path is exceedingly vast.

—O'Sensei

At the end of an aikido class, do you have the same high level of presence, skill, timing, and energy that you had when you first stepped onto the mat? Are you equally alert, exuberant, and ready to handle multiple attacks all class long? It's one thing to focus on one strike at a time; it's a different experience to be able to sustain that focus, flexibility, and responsiveness over time. Can you maintain that level over the course of a weekend aikido workshop or a weeklong seminar?

O'Sensei supposedly challenged his top students to attack him at any moment, 24 hours a day. When he was sharing a meal with his family, in his garden, while meditating, or when he was asleep, at no time did he take a break. Even as they silently crept up to O'Sensei in the middle of the night, at the last moment, he would quickly move out of a dead sleep before a strike found its target. They were never successful in their attempts. To watch O'Sensei demonstrate the art of aikido on the mat must have been impressive; to witness that same level of presence and skill around the clock surely was awe-inspiring.

One characteristic of the *randori principles* and effortless leadership is sustainability. Can you sustain high levels of performance, not just in the moment, but also over extended periods of time? Your pacing, use of resources, and relationships with colleagues are different when you have a long-term perspective, as opposed to a short-term focus. A flash of brilliance, a perfectly handled attack, or a hugely successful product launch, for example, is one thing. To deliver that level of performance *over time* requires a different mindset and skills.

On the mat, there are certain tactics that are important in achieving sustainability. The first approach is how you manage your energy. Your pacing dictates the use of just enough power as is required to deal with the attack, and nothing more. This means no showboating or "trashing" your opponent. Conversely, too little power doesn't neutralize the strike, and you end up expending more energy by the time that interaction is over. You balance delivering effective responses with conserving vital energy.

Second, you treat your adversaries differently when you know you will be interacting with them over the long term. You emphasize respect and not arrogance, knowing that they will be attacking many times over the upcoming years. For example, using excessive force in your technique predictably triggers revenge in their later attacks. Just because you are successful today doesn't mean that your colleagues won't be improving their skills. Over time, you can never underestimate your adversaries.

Paying attention to all the interactions on the mat, not just your incoming attacker, is the third tactic. Overly focusing on just one attack creates a blind spot for anticipating the next. Instead, watch all four attackers at the same time, and you will begin to see a pattern in their strikes. Expand your field of vision beyond your adversaries, and you will avoid throwing your attacker into the path of another aikidoist. When the mat is crowded, everyone takes responsibility for creating an environment of alertness and safety. It's not just about *your* practice.

When you manage your vital energy for the long term, you approach your colleagues as if you will be practicing together for many years and view your interactions in concert with all the other participants. From that place, you adopt an aikido practice style that is sustainable, whether for a weeklong seminar or a lifetime of classes.

Requiring the same tactics, sustainable leadership takes one moment of effortless action and extends that experience over time. The first tactic, managing the vital energy of your organization, goes against current business habits. Too often, business leaders take the attitude that if you don't spend your entire budget, you won't get as much next year. Another habit is to indiscriminately throw activity at a problem. If in doubt, start doing something, anything. Rarely are managers rewarded for choosing to not take action, to shut down, purposely to delay a project, or to conserve resources because the project justification or timing wasn't right. Instead, leaders need to balance the judicious selection of activity with the conservation of the vital energy of their organization.

The second sustainable leadership tactic is to view your actions as having long-term impact. Angeles Arrien suggests focusing on two questions when looking at the potential long-term impact you can have in the world: (1) Will this activity make the world a better place 100 years from now? (2) Are there sufficient resources being applied at this time? If not, that opportunity becomes a point of personal focus. If there are sufficient resources, choose another place to make a difference. Part of sustainability is carefully selecting where to devote your resources and keeping the long-term picture. Consider not just the next quarter or even the next several years but the long view.

Part of taking this long view is to view leadership decisions as part of a larger global context. Focus on specific projects but take into consideration the impact within the company, the industry, and a larger global environment. Consider interacting with competitors as if someday they may become business partners, suppliers as if they will be customers, and political adversaries as if you may have to work side by side to solve a global crisis in the future. This "both-and" attitude is crucial to sustainability.

The leader concerned with sustainability continually asks questions like:

How does each major project add value 5 years from now? How about 25 years? What purpose will your business serve in 100 years?

Where do I need to conserve the vital resources of my organization?

Which activities need to be accelerated, put on hold, or eliminated?

What can we do to enhance global relationships for future collaboration?

Randori teaches us that effortless leadership requires discernment, making decisions that create sustainable organizations and a global environment that can thrive over the next millennium. It's important to (1) eliminate activity that results in struggle and harm or projects that only add short-term value and (2) protect the vital energy of your team. The benefits of sustainability are prolonged results, availability of vital resources, and anticipation of future business challenges.

TRY THIS . . .

- Take out a sheet of paper.

- Draw two lines on it and take a hard and long look at the following two questions with the goal of preserving your company's vitality.

- Which activities need to be accelerated?

- Which need to be put on hold or eliminated?

JH

TODAY'S LEADERSHIP SKILLS WON'T BE GOOD ENOUGH TOMORROW

Learning is not filling a pail. It's lighting a fire.

—William Yeats

There is a videotape of O'Sensei rumored to exist in which ten men with live swords simultaneously attack him. As you follow the video frame by frame, you see him standing calmly inside a circle of armed attackers. As the images go by . . . forward movement . . . attack in progress . . . swords go up ready to strike . . . swords come down in full assault . . . then O'Sensei is suddenly gone. He is standing on the outside of the circle, smiling at his bewildered attackers who are confused and off balance in the middle. It is untrackable on film and unexplainable in science. But it happened, and the videotape shows something quite mysterious. When you watch the tape it seems so effortless. His grace and mastery are truly astounding.

And in that grace sits a trap.

There is a tendency to feel that effortless is the same as effort-free, and this is just not so. Mastery typically requires decades of focus, preparation, and practice; it is rarely something that one steps into. Tiger Woods's effortless swing did not just happen. Yes, he has a natural gift. That helps a lot. But the mastery of that gift was brought forward only with dedication and a lifelong commitment to golf—one

MOVING TO ADVANCED RANDORI

thing building on another until one day effortless mastery is achieved.

Jacob Riis, the famous photographer known for his seemingly unobtrusive shots of New York, said it best: "Look at a stonecutter hammering away at his rock. Perhaps a hundred times without as much as a crack showing in it. Yet at the hundred-and-first blow it will split in two, and I know it was not the last blow that did it, but all that had gone before."

As a leader, this focus is important to remember. The work you do in preparation *is* the work of effortless mastery. It is the commitment, during both easy and inconvenient times, that builds the base of effortless action.

A common error of senior leadership is to assume that once a level of power is achieved, focus on continued development is no longer needed. This is a mistake. Rank is not the same as effortless. The responsibility to your *randori* skill development will become stronger the higher you rise in your organization. After all, the more you can influence, the more you will want to do it responsibly and with minimal effort.

Jonathan Coslet, senior partner at Texas Pacific Investments, once told me: "When I became a senior partner I realized it was time to commit myself to truly developing my leadership skills. At my level it's all about leveraging talents. The difference between me being able to lead a $1 billion company versus a $7 billion company is all about developing effortless execution."

This is the full-hearted commitment needed to achieve effortless success—whether in business or on the mat. The intention toward one's long-term disciplined growth, especially when age or position or power implies it is no longer needed, is the secret to avoiding sword attacks—especially those occurring in the boardroom.

Said another way, when Pablo Casals, the great cellist, reached 95, a young reporter once asked him: "Mr. Casals, you are 95 and the greatest cellist who ever lived. Why do you still practice six hours a day?" Casals answered, "Because I think I'm still making progress."

TRY THIS . . .

- Ask yourself, "Do I have a self-development plan in place for my career vision?"

- If not (and most don't), tap five to ten people you trust for their ideas on what are your greatest needs as a leader.

- Then use that information as the basis for moving forward.

DB

AVOID OVERDEPENDENCE ON LEADERSHIP

"Come to the edge," he said.
They said, "We are afraid."
"Come to the edge," he said.
They came. He pushed them. And they flew.

—Guillaume Apollinaire

Have you ever seen pictures of those gigantic ten-foot termite mounds in Africa? They are truly marvels of engineering and cooperation. These mounds are huge, magnificent structures, built by creatures so small that a similar human structure would dwarf anything currently on the planet.

What's amazing to note, however, is that this entire fantastic effort is done *without a leader*. Termites have no hierarchy like ants to direct or manage. Every termite is an equal, performing a task for the common good.

They create this monumental structure by following three simple rules that are never violated:

Rule 1. Every termite keeps moving till it finds a piece of wood.

Rule 2. When it finds a piece of wood, it picks it up and keeps moving.

Rule 3. When it finds another piece of wood, it drops the one it has, leaving a small pile, and goes back to rule one.

By this process, termites end up creating one of the greatest engineering marvels on the planet.

There are many lessons to be taken from this extraordinary feat, but one bears additional attention. It is this: Great leaders are careful not to create overdependence on their leadership.

This means knowing that leadership is sometimes not called for. A great leader knows when and how to step back, and when his power as a leader limits and colludes to a weakened workforce. Great leadership recognizes both the inherent value and the limitations of one's abilities.

As a leader, you need to create processes that teach your people to step up to the next level. This process does *not* need to be complex. Remember the termites? They're bugs, not MIT engineers. But these simple insects create a structure we humans have yet to be able to duplicate with all our scientific resources. Their genius is in a simple model that minimizes complexity, while allowing outcome through process rather than leadership personality.

To be an advanced *randori* leader means setting up processes that sustain far beyond your personal involvement and leading in ways in which you are not the central figure. Advanced *randori* leadership asks, "What should you *not* be doing?" Said another way, "Where is your leadership getting in the way of your people?" This typically arises in leaders who tend to overcontrol a situation or team, sticking their fingers into every pie.

This can be especially challenging to charismatic leaders who motivate and inspire through the strength of their personality. And when the lesson comes, it can be humbling.

Here's an example: Chris Rich is a successful and well-regarded attorney in Salem, Massachusetts. A few years ago, he started suffering from dizzy spells. After seeing his doctor, he was told shocking news. He had 13 brain lesions that needed immediate surgery.

He told me the following outcome: "Before my surgery I was—well, let's not be delicate—I was a major prick! I was thoughtless, inconsiderate, and a micromanager of my business. I was a very difficult person to work for. But at the start of my seven operations, I began to change. It became physically impossible for me to manage my business in the same way. I couldn't concentrate, couldn't read, and couldn't do any of the things I traditionally did as a leader. Out of physical necessity, I was forced to trust my people's capacity to deliver. As a consequence, I delegated the business downward.

"During recovery, my brother came to visit me in the hospital.

"Solemnly, he said, 'We need to talk about the business.' This was not good. The look on his face told me the news would not be pleasant. I could feel myself starting to explode, even though I was warned to avoid any stress.

"He handed me two sheets of paper and said, 'On the first sheet are the numbers when you ran the business. The second sheet shows how the business has been doing since you've been out.' Then he took a long pause, enough time for me to read the figures, and said, 'You might want to think about staying out!'"

It is a frequent story for strong and competent leaders who create dependency with their people. In essence, the leader stunts growth, development, and risk taking through his "compassionate guidance." His people will sit on the sidelines and wait for direction, wait for the boss to solve a crisis rather than initiate of their own accord.

Don't get us wrong. We are all for strong leadership. But, like any issue taken out of balance, a heavy price is paid when leadership is overused. Many books are written about how and when to use leadership effectively. Little consideration is ever given to when *not* to lead. It is the mark of deep leadership wisdom to know that, regardless of how well intentioned, your presence will sometimes hinder through meddling or dependency.

We ask you to consider the wise mantra of our friend Peggy Cappy, who says, "I want to help . . . but not too much."

TRY THIS . . .

- Find a picture of a termite colony in Africa. Put it over your desk.

- Whenever you find yourself wanting to jump into a situation, remember the lesson of the termite colony. Your presence to fix the problem may be overrated.

- Ask yourself, "Is there a better way to do this in which I am not involved?"

DB

TAKE A DEEP DIVE INTO
EFFORTLESS LEADERSHIP

You are the same today that you are going to be five years
from now except for two things: the people with whom
you associate and the actions you take.

—Unknown

Recently, I returned from a diving trip to the Cayman Islands. During my stay, I met four members of the Canadian Free Dive Team. Free diving is the art of staying underwater and/or going deep without the benefit of an air source. It's no different really from what you used to do as a kid. Just take a breath on the surface and see if you can touch bottom or stay under longer than your friends. Competitive diving is done at another level (Canada placed second in the 2000 world team championships).

The first afternoon I saw them training in the pool, they were doing static breath-holding exercises. They'd take a breath, hold it, bend over into a facedown float, and start counting. Some were going over five and a half minutes— *without air.* It was an amazing thing to witness.

On the last day of our vacation, my stepdaughter Kate and I decided to take a class in free diving to see what we could learn. I never imagined I would be able to come remotely close in skill level. I can barely hold my breath for 30 seconds, and picking up a quarter on the bottom of a pool at a depth of nine feet is a big challenge. But an incredible thing happened. After some lessons in proper breath preparation and the right techniques for diving, we were holding our breath for two minutes and touching bottom at 35 feet! And that was after a few hours. One diver told us a three-minute breath hold and 50 feet was well within our grasp with a little practice. Granted, three minutes is a breeze compared to the five and a half I witnessed, and 50 feet is a far cry from the 260 feet plus they do, but I left the Caymans with visions of Aquaman running through my head. The lesson was clear: Our beliefs and personal limits can be expanded far beyond our assumptions with proper training and focus.

As in free diving, the same is also true for putting the *randori principles* into practice. As a leader interested in application, the requirements are the same. What's called for, above all else, is a willingness to try.

When Jim and I started to write *The Randori Principles,* I knew very little about aikido. I had over twenty years of experience with organizational change and leadership, but aikido? Not really. My expertise extended to little more than a topical exposure from seeing a few Steven Segal films. It was a concept, not a practice.

However, early on I began to challenge my own self-imposed aikido limitations. Although I am pretty confident this art will never become a lifelong passion for me like it is for Jim, in some ways it doesn't matter. I have begun to incorporate the philosophy of aikido into my daily life and that, more than anything, has made a huge difference in my own "effortless" leadership. I believe the beliefs and principles of aikido have as much relevance to me as they do for a sixth-degree Black Belt. And I can apply the lessons with incredible effectiveness to improve as a manager, advisor, and even husband and father. The *randori principles* just work.

We fully encourage you to try some of these concepts. *Randori* cannot be learned from the sidelines. You must get on the metaphorical mat. This requires, above all else, the courage to try something new, and if necessary, dive into uncharted waters. Try thinking big, maybe beyond your sense of what is possible for yourself as a leader. By taking this full and strong-hearted commitment to action, the path to effortless leadership is more than within your grasp. It can be within your nature.

So take a deep breath. As Phillip Brooks once said, "Do not pray for dreams equal to your powers. Pray for powers equal to your dreams."

TRY THIS . . .

- Go through the book and select three application tips to put into action.

- There's no magic here. Time to get out of the book and onto the mat.

- Just do it.

DB

SUGGESTED READING LIST

To learn more about the concepts outlined in this book, we suggest the following:

Arrien, Angeles. *The Four-Fold Way: Walking the Paths of the Warrior, Teacher, Healer, and Visionary*. San Francisco: Harper San Francisco, 1993.

Baum, David. *Lightning in a Bottle: Proven Lessons for Leading Change*. Chicago: Dearborn Trade, 2000.

Bridges, William. *The Way of Transition: Embracing Life's Most Difficult Moments*. New York: Perseus Books, 2000.

Crum, Thomas. *The Magic of Conflict*. New York: Touchstone, 1987.

Dobson, Terry, Riki Moss, and Jan Watson. *It's a Lot Like Dancing: An Aikido Journal*. Frog Ltd., 1994.

Leonard, George. *Mastery: The Keys to Success and Long-Term Fulfillment*. New York: Penguin Putnam, 1992.

Moon, Richard. *Aikido in Three Easy Lessons.* Self-published, 1996.

Stevens, John, and Peter Turner, eds. *The Shambala Guide to Aikido.* Boston: Shambala Publications, 1996.

Ueshiba, Kisshomaru. *The Spirit of Aikido.* New York: Kodansha International, 1984.

Ueshiba, Morihei. *The Art of Peace.* Trans. John Stevens. Boston: Shambala Publications, 1992.